"**Chasing Hope** is a GPS for any famil̨
needs. Written by a parent on the jour.
not only hope to parents, but simple, e̟
steps to be part of policy ̟

—Former Congressman John Edward Porter
Founder of the Congressional Human Rights Caucus
Former chairman of PBS and Trustee Emeritus,
JFK Center for the Performing Arts

*Author's note: John Edward Porter served in Congress for 21 years,
representing the 10th district of Illinois. During his tenure, Porter served
on the House Appropriations Committee and for a time chaired the
Subcommittee which funded health research and mental health services
within the federal government. The John Edward Porter Neuroscience
Research Center at the National Institutes of Health is named in his honor.*

"*Christine Walker's* **Chasing Hope** *presents a candid portrayal of an
ongoing journey. The trip chronicles her emotion-filled experiences
related to seeking answers and solutions for her son who has
significant disabilities.* **Chasing Hope** *honestly addresses the
sadness, disappointment, frustration, and anger. It also captures
the hope and happiness associated with her son. This book, which
highlights extensive and exhaustive searching, offers tremendous
insights to families with children with significant needs.* **Chasing
Hope** *should be read by all parents, educators, and physicians.*"

—Dr. Tim Thomas
Northern Suburban Special Education District Superintendent

"*The Zen philosopher Alan Watts echoed the wisdom I've gleaned
from the lake. 'The only way to make sense out of change,' he said,
'is to plunge into it, move with it, and join the dance.'*"

—Phil Jackson (quoting Alan Watts)
11-time NBA championship and Hall of Fame coach

"**Chasing Hope** is not only a resource for families with children with autism and mental illness, but for policy makers as well. Schuyler's story illustrates a serious policy failure. Mrs. Walker's willingness to share her family's story in such an authentic manner is exceptional, and exemplifies the fearlessness she has shown throughout Schuyler's journey. The resolution of policy failures is only possible when brave families, like the Walkers, give voice to the issues. That Mrs. Walker had to become an expert in Schuyler's condition and the policy options available is heartbreaking, but her commitment to sharing the knowledge she acquired will undeniably help countless families."

—Dr. Angela Fontes
Northwestern University

"As a health professional and parent of a child with ASD I found myself reliving many of the emotions and feelings that were evoked by this book. The struggle to get the right diagnosis and treatment will strike a cord with parents. Some of the writing was so true to life that it raised the hairs on the back of my neck; reading about how driven a parent can become in this situation was fantastic. The lack of help for these children is an international problem and it is important for health professionals, policy makers, and other parents to hear such stories so that further action can be taken to improve help for future generations. I would encourage everyone who has an interest in this area to read this account and to reflect on the issues raised."

—Dr. Khalid Karim
Senior Clinical Teaching Fellow, University of Leicester, England
Consultant Child and Adolescent Psychiatrist, Leicestershire Partnership Trust, Leicester, England

CHASING HOPE

THE ORP
LIBRARY

We hope that you find this book from
<u>The ORP Library</u> valuable.

If this book touched you in a way that
you would be willing to share, we
encourage you to visit www.Amazon.com
or www.BN.com and write a short review.

www.ORPLibrary.com

CHASING HOPE
YOUR COMPASS
FOR A NEW NORMAL

NAVIGATING THE WORLD
OF THE SPECIAL NEEDS CHILD

THE ORP LIBRARY

WRITTEN BY

CHRISTINE WALKER, MPPA

WRITERS OF THE ROUND TABLE PRESS
PO BOX 511
HIGHLAND PARK, IL 60035

Publisher	COREY MICHAEL BLAKE
Executive Editor	KATIE GUTIERREZ
Staff Editor	PAMELA DELOATCH
Creative Director	DAVID CHARLES COHEN
Directoress of Happiness	ERIN COHEN
Director of Operations	KRISTIN WESTBERG
Facts Keeper	MIKE WINICOUR
Cover Design	ANALEE PAZ
Interior Design and Layout	SUNNY DIMARTINO
Proofreading	RITA HESS
Last Looks	SUNNY DIMARTINO
Digital Book Conversion	SUNNY DIMARTINO
Digital Publishing	SUNNY DIMARTINO

Printed in the United States of America
First Edition: March 2014
10 9 8 7 6 5 4 3 2 1

Library of Congress Cataloging-in-Publication Data
Walker, Christine
Chasing hope: your compass for a new normal /
Christine Walker.—1st ed. p. cm.
Print ISBN: 978-1-939418-50-0 Digital ISBN: 978-1-939418-51-7
Library of Congress Control Number: 2014935258
Number 8 in the series: The ORP Library
The ORP Library: Chasing Hope

RTC Publishing is an imprint of Writers of the Round Table, Inc.
Writers of the Round Table Press and the RTC Publishing logo
are trademarks of Writers of the Round Table, Inc.

CONTENTS

This book was inspired by my son, Schuyler, for whom God thought I would be a good mom. I can only hope that I live up to those expectations and am forgiven when I fall short. The book is dedicated to my family, whose courage, love, and support on our collective and unexpected journey sustains me. I hope that our family's truth comforts and strengthens your own family.

"*Start where you are. Use what you have.*
Do what you can."
—Arthur Ashe

INTRODUCTION BY JIM BALESTRIERI

Today, according to the U.S. Department of Health and Human Services, more than 5.5 million children—or eight percent of kids—in the U.S. have some form of disability. Whether the problem is physical, behavioral, or emotional, these children struggle to communicate, learn, and relate to others. While there is no longer *segregation* in the same sense as there was in the 1950s, what remains the same is the struggle. Even with all of our resources and technology, parents of children with disabilities fight battles every day to find the help and education their children need.

I have led Oconomowoc Residential Programs (ORP) for almost thirty years. We're a family of companies offering specialized services and care for children, adolescents, and adults with disabilities. Too often, when parents of children with disabilities try to find funding for programs like ours, they are bombarded by red tape, conflicting information, or no information at all, so they struggle blindly for years to secure an appropriate education. Meanwhile, home life, and the child's wellbeing, suffers. In cases when parents and caretakers have exhausted their options—and their hope—ORP is here to help. We felt it was time to offer parents a new, unexpected tool to fight back: stories that educate, empower, and inspire.

The original idea was to create a library of comic books that could empower families with information to reclaim their rights. We wanted to give parents and caretakers the information they need to advocate for themselves, as well as provide educators and therapists with a therapeutic tool. And, of course, we wanted to reach the children—to offer them a visual representation of their journey that would show that they aren't alone, nor are they wrong or "bad" for their differences. What we found in the process of writing original stories for the comics is that these journeys are too long, too complex, to be contained within a standard comic. So what we are now creating is an ORP library of disabilities books—traditional books geared toward parents, caretakers, educators, and therapists, *and* comic books portraying the world through the eyes of children with disabilities. Both styles of books share what we have learned while advocating for families over the years while also honestly highlighting their emotional journeys. We're creating communication devices that anyone can read to understand complex disabilities in a new way.

In an ideal situation, these books will be used therapeutically, to communicate the message, and to help support the work ORP and companies like ours are doing. The industry has changed dramatically and is not likely to turn around any time soon—certainly not without more people being aware of families' struggles. We have an opportunity to put a face to the conversation, reach out to families, and start that dialogue.

Caring for children with disabilities consumes your life. We know that. And we want you to realize, through these stories, that you are not alone. We can help.

Sincerely,
Jim Balestrieri
CEO, Oconomowoc Residential Programs
www.orplibrary.com

INTRODUCTION BY CHRISTINE WALKER

Two days before Christmas 2004, I sat in the child psychiatrist's office and finally received our four-year-old son's diagnosis: our beautiful boy, Schuyler, had bipolar II disorder, autism, and ADHD. The devastating conclusion came after more than two and a half years of seeking answers and assistance, of my gut screaming that something wasn't right with our son, and of wondering when all of it would get better.

Before Schuyler was born in 2000, my jobs as a legislative aide and corporate sales coach required that I excel at problem solving. Once I received his diagnosis, I thought my background would prepare me to conquer this challenge. I didn't yet realize that the diagnosis was only the beginning.

After leaving the doctor's office that day, I immediately launched into The Search: a quest for that ONE thing that was going to make it all better. I called doctors, psychiatrists, occupational therapists, speech pathologists, chiropractors, nutrition specialists, pediatric neurologists, authors, and our local special education district, hoping that someone, anyone, would give us a definitive answer. What WAS this? What did Schuyler's diagnoses mean for his future? How could we help him? Despite reaching out to every expert who would listen, nothing made a dent. Schuyler's behavior did not improve, and in some cases, it got worse. Schuyler's lack of speech, his tantrums, and his aggression led to two different preschool programs asking us to leave in the span of five months. I was exhausted, harried, confused, angry, and sad. I was also going broke and could feel my marriage weakening.

My husband, Dave, and I had been married almost two years before Schuyler was born. Dave and I met in Connecticut at a polo match, when I was on a business trip to New York and Dave was working there in sales. I was attracted to his charm and kindness. The connection was immediate, and commuting only made us more determined to be together. A year after we met, we got married, and Dave continued commuting for six months until he was able to move to Chicago. By the time we received Schuyler's diagnoses, Dave was the manager of a boutique investment firm. He worked long hours and traveled a lot, driven by his own quest to achieve and a desire to provide for his family. But as a result, I felt he was not as engaged in what was happening with Schuyler. When he was confronted with the problems, he either minimized them or denied that they existed.

Our family, which would eventually include two younger children, was on a massive hamster wheel, running in panic mode in search of a remedy that would relieve Schuyler's challenges as well as lessen some of the horridness of daily life in our home. I convinced myself that the next doctor, the next diet, the next medication, the next speaker, the next treatment, the next *whatever* would make Schuyler well.

One night, as I was heading out to hear yet another presentation on what medical miracle was around the corner, Dave asked where I was going. I shouted, "I'm chasing hope! Be back around nine."

Each day was chaos. Every roadblock we hit seemed insurmountable, every stressor became a health risk, and every "character builder" seemed like one more burden that we couldn't or didn't know how to manage. I wished that someone who had gone through what I was going through would just take me out for coffee and tell me certain truths about this journey. I needed candid, real-world straight talk about what I was dealing with. Instead, I got referrals to nine (yes, nine) different clinicians "to see what they said" about Schuyler. Insurance wasn't paying for much, if any, of these treatments or sessions. What's more, I found that in some cases, I was teaching the "expert" more about Schuyler's behavior and how we managed it than the expert was sharing with me. And I paid ninety-five dollars a session for the privilege.

The idea of someone giving me straight advice reminded me of one of my favorite books, Maria Shriver's *Ten Things I Wish I'd Known Before I Went Out into the Real World*. Shriver's work began as a speech to a graduating class at Holy Cross, and her words were straightforward and un-sugarcoated. The speech became a book, expanding on the experiences behind the wisdom shared that day. In it, Shriver is candid about the life lessons she learned, many of them the hard way, after leaving college. In essence, her message was, "Here is what I wish someone had told me when I was sitting where you are."

Like Shriver, there are at least ten things I wish someone had told me when Schuyler's behavior first appeared at the age of eighteen months. Having that knowledge would have allowed me to get through those next few years in a better frame of mind. It is with that same spirit that I decided to create a handbook of sorts that any parent of a child with special needs can turn to for guidance, support, laughter, and plain straight talk that doctors and other professionals rarely provide. These stories are meant to offer help and hope, not to mention the straight dope on the challenges of everyday living: parents' efforts to find a cure, choose a course of treatment, hunt down scientists, pursue authors and researchers, all while trying to manage their lives and their health while keeping their families intact.

But this book is not just to commiserate with you. My goal is to provide some specific, tangible actions that you can take to make a difference in your child's life and your family's life, including how your participation in the law-making process greatly impacts how conditions, diseases, and behaviors are treated. Have you heard the phrase *hell hath no fury like a woman scorned*? That woman has nothing on the parent of a sick child! There are ways to focus your energy on making the world a better place, even if it is just the world of your home, block, or city.

Learning that your child has a disability probably represented a huge detour in your expectations of parenthood. When you were younger and thought about getting married and raising a family, you probably didn't imagine this, right? On the day you found out you were expecting, did you have visions of pushing a stroller in the park and smiling? Did you pick out picture frames from Pottery Barn Kids that you planned to use for the cute First Day of School photo? And did your conversations with friends and neighbors swirl around visions of playmates and prom dates? Or did you see yourself needing to become a walking *Physicians' Desk Reference*? Did you even know what an IEP was before this child came into your life?

Emily Perl Kingsley, a writer for Sesame Street and an author of children's books, wrote an essay about having a child with a disability. Titled *Welcome to Holland*, it asks you to imagine that you've anticipated and meticulously planned for a trip to Italy. You've prepared mentally and physically for your time in that specific place, only to find that your flight was irreversibly diverted to Holland. Holland is not what you expected. It's not what you planned for. It doesn't have the food you craved or art you came to see. It's not, dang it, what you wanted. But, after realizing it is what it is, you begin to look around your new surroundings. You find that Holland is different from Italy—not better or worse, just different. And once you get over being upset that you are not in Italy, you somehow begin to see that Holland isn't so bad after all. In fact, Holland has a specialness and beauty of its own.

Just as described in that essay, at the heart of chasing hope is acceptance: acceptance of your child and his or her condition, acceptance of your new normalcy and success redefined, and acceptance that despite this tremendous curve ball thrown at your head, you will be okay.

Welcome to Holland.

> *"Everything that is done in the world*
> *is done by hope."*
> —Martin Luther

WELCOME TO HOLLAND

I am often asked to describe the experience of raising a child with a disability—to try to help people who have not shared that unique experience to understand it, to imagine how it would feel. It's like this . . .

When you're going to have a baby, it's like planning a fabulous vacation trip—to Italy. You buy a bunch of guide books and make your wonderful plans. The Coliseum. The Michelangelo David. The gondolas in Venice. You may learn some handy phrases in Italian. It's all very exciting.

After months of eager anticipation, the day finally arrives. You pack your bags and off you go. Several hours later, the plane lands. The flight attendant comes in and says, "Welcome to Holland."

"Holland?!?" you say. "What do you mean Holland?? I signed up for Italy! I'm supposed to be in Italy. All my life I've dreamed of going to Italy."

But there's been a change in the flight plan. They've landed in Holland and there you must stay.

The important thing is that they haven't taken you to a horrible, disgusting, filthy place, full of pestilence, famine and disease. It's just a different place.

So you must go out and buy new guide books. And you must learn a whole new language. And you will meet a whole new group of people you would never have met.

It's just a different place. It's slower-paced than Italy, less flashy than Italy. But after you've been there for a while and you catch your breath, you look around . . . and you begin to notice *that Holland has windmills . . . and Holland has tulips. Holland even has Rembrandts.*

But everyone you know is busy coming and going from Italy . . . and they're all bragging about what a wonderful time they had there. And for the rest of your life, you will say "Yes, that's where I was supposed to go. That's what I had planned."

And the pain of that will never, ever, ever, ever go away . . . because the loss of that dream is a very, very significant loss.

But . . . if you spend your life mourning the fact that you didn't get to Italy, you may never be free to enjoy the very special, the very lovely things . . . about Holland.

A NOTE ABOUT THIS BOOK

While many books are available about helping a child with special needs, very few have addressed the family's perspective of helping a child thrive with a mental illness. Often considered a hidden epidemic, one out of every five children in the United States experiences a mental disorder each year. Some, like Schuyler, the boy in this book, spend years seeking diagnosis. Once a diagnosis is reached, families still struggle to find a balance of treatment and effective resources. Even today, mental illness is not completely understood, but we hope this book increases awareness, understanding, and compassion while providing down-to-earth guidance for parents who are chasing hope for their children.

"Never deprive someone of hope;
it might be all they have."
—H. Jackson Brown, Jr.

CHAPTER 1
THE CALL FROM REALITY

As a first-time parent of a preschooler, I had no idea that when a teacher pulls you aside during pickup and asks when might be a good time to talk, it's not a good thing.

Schuyler, often shortened to Sky, had been enrolled at the Montessori school for just a few weeks. As a child, I had gone to a Montessori school, and Dave and I both felt that this kind of school would be great for our son. The Montessori style of education is based on the idea of child-centered learning. A child will learn at his pace, exploring the areas that interest him the most. This sounded perfect for a little boy who sometimes struggled with structure. At two years old, Schuyler wasn't talking yet; instead, his communication (when he wasn't screaming or crying) was more like grunting and pointing, but at his recent checkup, his pediatrician assured me that some boys just talk later. I was almost due with my second son, Connor, and wondered if somehow Schuyler sensed the changes that a sibling would bring and was acting out in some way. Either way, Dave and I thought that surely the activity at preschool and the interaction with other children would help calm Schuyler's behavior.

In addition to not talking, Schuyler became frustrated very easily, melting down into tantrums that had him kicking and screaming on the floor, or he would suddenly fall apart if the feel of his clothes aggravated him or if he had to walk on grass or sand barefoot. Maybe the frustration occurred because Schuyler couldn't express himself. In time, we hoped, everything would work itself out.

For months, we had planned and saved to send Schuyler to this Montessori school. Just three blocks from our house, its playground was our playground once the students had gone home each day. Schuyler's eyes lit up whenever we entered its gates. He especially loved the sand pit that had an excavator for digging and a huge train engine he could sit in. We already loved the school. I didn't want just a daycare for Schuyler. I wanted him to be engaged and enriched, taught by teachers who understood child development. But three weeks into the year, the phone call came as expected after his teacher asked to talk.

"Mrs. Walker, I'm concerned about something," the teacher said hesitantly. "Schuyler is still not talking, but he is also disruptive. He hurls toys and throws tantrums when it's time to move from one activity to another." After a brief pause, she added, "I don't think this is working out."

Her words took a moment to sink in. Then I sputtered, "But it's just been a few weeks! He's only two and has never gone to school before. Wouldn't it help to give him a little more time to settle in and be around the teachers and other kids?"

Schuyler's teacher sighed, and we set up a time to come in after school the next day and make a plan for the coming weeks.

The next evening, Dave and I met with Schuyler's teacher, as well as the administrator of the Montessori school. In the office, the administrator sat down across from us at her desk. Dave and I sat side by side, with me feeling as though we were in a physician's office about to get some bad test results.

"What exactly is the problem?" I asked, hoping that the answers would not crush me. I looked hopefully at Schuyler's teacher. She had been teaching at Montessori for twenty years and had the combination of calmness and energy that indicated she could lovingly handle active children. When I first met her, I immediately felt at ease, knowing that she might be able to reach Schuyler in such a way that the challenges we had been having would be a thing of the past. Now, however, she wouldn't look directly at me.

The administrator glanced at the teacher, then back at me. "I'm afraid that Schuyler's needs exceed our resources."

"What does that mean?" I asked.

The administrator pressed her lips together but looked at me sympathetically. "I'm sorry, Mrs. Walker. It's just not the right fit. He has not adjusted well here, and we think it would be best for Schuyler if he were to leave."

Leave? Since when was leaving a plan? I thought we might talk about how to be consistent with rules at home that were used at school or about me coming to observe him, but for him to get kicked out of preschool?

"But what about . . ." The words began to trip from my lips. I wanted to problem solve and look for solutions that would make this work, but as I looked at the unyielding expressions on their faces, my voice trailed off. I could

3

see that their decision had been made and that this conversation was simply a courtesy. I glanced at Dave, who looked as dumbstruck as I felt, and sat there in silence for a moment, absorbing the blow.

"So there's no other way?" Dave asked finally.

"I'm afraid not," the administrator confirmed.

My shock was transitioning to anger: Schuyler obviously wasn't welcomed here. I needed to find another school that would want Schuyler to be a part of their family.

With my mind already racing, I began planning the transition. I could start calling preschools in the morning to find out if they had availabilities, and by the end of the week, perhaps, I'd withdraw Schuyler from the Montessori school. Next week, he could start somewhere new.

"All right," Dave said. "When should Schuyler plan to leave the school?"

"I suggest that tomorrow be his last day," the administrator said. "That way, he can say goodbye to his classmates."

Tomorrow? Wow. That was quite a message. My face felt hot as I struggled to contain my emotions. I was angry at how the school seemed so quick to dismiss a child who didn't fit into their box; curious that his behavior had been too challenging for a staff that prided itself on child-guided and exploratory learning; and sad that my first experience as the parent of a student had ended so soon after it began. After tomorrow, even if we came to play on the playground, we wouldn't truly belong.

"Mrs. Walker," the administrator called to me as Dave and I headed for the door. "You might not want to enroll Schuyler in another program right away, because the same thing is likely to happen. Maybe his pediatrician can make some recommendations for a place that is more equipped to handle him."

I remember telling myself to wait until I got in the car to cry.

On shaky legs, I walked out the door and into the parking lot. Dave opened the passenger door of our car and I sank into the seat, resting my head on the seat back.

"What was that?" he asked, bewildered.

I shook my head, trying but failing to squeeze the tears back.

I knew Schuyler could be a handful, but he could also be so sweet, so loving, and so smart. We could have a spell of about a week and half where everything went smoothly. Sky would easily stop playing with cars to come eat lunch. He'd wake up from his afternoon nap feeling cheerful and ready to go to the park. But other days, anything could set him off. He could wake up from his afternoon nap crying inconsolably or have a meltdown if we couldn't go to the park because it was raining. He was unpredictable, but he was as deserving of a quality preschool as any other child.

Despite the administrator's caution, within a few months, I found another preschool for Schuyler. By this time, Connor was two months old, and not only did I want Schuyler to get a little enrichment, but I also needed a break during the day so I could care for a newborn. I found a sweet little church program that wasn't as sophisticated as Montessori, but the staff was made up of grandmotherly types who seemed to genuinely love the kids. Schuyler was the only boy in a class of ten. While the girls could sit still and draw or make glitter projects for a long time, Sky repeatedly made messes and caused chaos, throwing toys in the air and watching them land everywhere. It took this school two, maybe three, months to ask Schuyler to leave.

When one school asked my two-year-old to leave, I could blame it on him not fitting in. I could say the teachers didn't "get" active little boys. But when two schools asked him to leave, I knew in my gut that something wasn't right. But I also didn't have any answers or even know the right questions to ask to get them. All I could wonder was, *What is going on with Schuyler?*

. . .

When Schuyler was a baby, life was sweet. Sometimes I thumb through photos of the three of us—Schuyler, Dave, and me—and I see the happiness on our faces. I see our contentment, our absolute bliss. It makes me sad, though, to remember those carefree, happy times. They were over so quickly.

We took Schuyler to London with us when he was just six months old, getting him his own passport. He went with us everywhere, comfortably tucked into the baby carrier, including afternoon tea at The Ritz and strolls through museums—he was a total champ! One of my favorite photos of that trip is the three of us standing in the familiar red telephone booth with Big Ben in the background. Schuyler seemed genuinely happily to tag along. On the flights there and back, he didn't fuss at all and took to napping on the floor of the plane between my feet, lulled to sleep by the vibrations.

As Schuyler grew, though, his behavior wasn't even the typical "boy" behavior that some of my friends described. Some boys enjoyed making a mess. Schuyler enjoyed creating chaos.

"Schuyler, put that sand down!" I called to him at the playground. One of his favorite activities was to throw sand, and when another child got upset, it seemed to spur Schuyler into throwing even more sand.

"James, come here," another mother called to her son, beckoning him away from Schuyler.

I couldn't blame her. Other children would walk away from playing with Schuyler when he became frustrated at waiting for a turn on the slide or sharing beach toys. Mothers looked at me with indictment in their eyes, wondering why I didn't have a better handle on Schuyler's behavior. The truth is, we tried everything. We tried positive reinforcement, with stickers and reminders, but when he was too deep in the spiral of destruction, he couldn't seem to stop himself. No sooner had I gotten Connor settled down in his crib at home than I'd hear Schuyler throwing toy cars against the walls and windows.

"Schuyler, if you throw those toys like that, you'll dent the wall," I explained to him. I pointed out several dings already on the wall of his bedroom. Schuyler looked up at me, angelic curls ringing his head. Then he threw another toy car against the window, shattering the glass. When I gasped, he laughed. His face was giddy. Even hearing the disapproval in my voice wouldn't deter him. In fact, it seemed to energize him.

Schuyler took all of the Tupperware bowls and lids out of the kitchen cabinets, flinging them across the room, laughing louder with each throw. Linen closets were another favorite play place. There, he took every folded sheet and towel off the shelf and threw it down the hallway. Same with the changing table in both his room and Connor's. Diapers that were stacked in rows became small piles all over the floor. The pants and Onesies that were folded and ready for any change or accident that might occur were lumped in the corners of the room. I told myself that this was typical toddler behavior and not to worry about it. But it was the *pleasure* that Schuyler took in creating the chaos that concerned me. It wasn't just that he was enjoying this; he seemed almost driven to do this, as if he couldn't stop himself.

"Why did you do that?" I would ask, somehow expecting him to answer me in full sentences. He smiled. The angrier I got, the more gleeful Schuyler became. He seemed to refuel from the frustration and pandemonium he caused. Throwing Tupperware and diapers was inconvenient, even seemingly harmless, but sometimes, his tantrums scared me. One day, we were leaving one of his favorite places, a ball pit, and getting into the car. Schuyler didn't want to interrupt his play, and he struggled mightily in my arms, screaming and kicking, even as I buckled him into his car seat. He reached as far as he could and hurled every object he could touch, his face beet red and sweating. Any kid can have a tantrum now and then, but more often, when they didn't get their way, they might cry or pout. Schuyler could go into full-scale rages that were unstoppable until he finally exhausted himself and fell asleep. With him safely strapped inside the car, I closed the door and stood outside, taking deep breaths. *What two-year-old does that? And what will happen if I'm driving and Schuyler throws something at me or at Connor, who might be sitting next to him?*

I still didn't know what was going on with Schuyler, but I knew one thing for sure: something was wrong.

"The capacity for hope is the most significant fact of life. It provides human beings with a sense of destination and the energy to get started."
—Norman Cousins

"There is a crack in everything.
That's how the light gets in."
—Leonard Cohen

CHAPTER 2
A SOLITARY JOURNEY

Looking at Schuyler, with his bright smile and tight hugs, my heart ached as I realized that despite all of the dismissals and possibilities I had given and been given for his behavior, something was truly wrong with him. Two preschools had asked him to leave. What made his behavior, out of all of the terrible two-year-old antics, so extreme?

After I recovered from the initial shock of Schuyler being a preschool dropout, I didn't know what to do. My heart could not handle the possibility of being kicked out of yet another preschool, so I opted to keep Schuyler at home. Since we were no longer tethered to a daily school routine, we had time to spend on nailing down answers as to exactly what the hell we had on our hands. And so I set out on what would be a very long and very lonely road.

Schuyler's lack of speech was a huge part of the problem. Just about every professional said that not being able to talk was the reason for Schuyler's behavior, adding that his level of frustration would increase with each obstacle he encountered.

"Why don't you check out the speech and language program at Northwestern University?" our pediatrician suggested. Our pediatrician was on the staff of Northwestern's medical school and was familiar with the testing and diagnostics available to families, so I made an appointment and went to have Schuyler evaluated.

The morning of the first batch of tests was for language and speech, and as we walked into the Searle Building on Northwestern's Evanston campus, I was unsure of what to expect. With now six-month-old Connor in tow, I settled into the couch in the waiting lounge to tackle a ten-page parent intake form. How was my pregnancy? Were there any medical conditions? Any family history of neurological disorders? Good God. Really? Schuyler had as great a start in life as one could ever hope for. *Why are you asking this?* I wondered. As I made my way down the list of questions, it struck me that I could not answer any of the ones related to Dave's family history. Dave was adopted as an infant and does not have any information about his birth parents. This black hole of information would prove to be another source of contention in our marriage, as many times I felt as though Dave placed the blame on me and on my side of the family, which had a history of brain disorders. Over the years, Dave would repeatedly tell me that he never meant to imply any blame, and in hindsight, I believe him, though it was a very painful time. Having just celebrated our fifteenth wedding anniversary, we're still working on truly resolving the hurt feelings that resulted from this.

The first batch of tests ruled out any physical limitations to speech. They couldn't find any for Schuyler.

The second battery of tests involved Schuyler's hearing.

The audiologist told me that during these speech and language evaluations, they needed to rule out any hearing loss as an underlying cause. Please! Schuyler could hear a commuter train coming from the next stop. He could probably hear dog whistles, too. Half an hour later, yep, hearing was perfect! Check hearing loss off the list. (I had checked that off a while ago myself, for free.)

After the initial observations, testing, reviewing my intake answers, and performing what seemed like an inquisition, the director of the speech and language center confirmed that, yes, Schuyler did officially have a speech delay. I knew that while Schuyler could understand what was being said (receptive language), he could not initiate conversation (expressive language). In other words, Schuyler would walk over to a table of books and point to the one he wanted; he just couldn't explicitly *say* what he needed. So what could we do about it?

"He would definitely benefit from seeing a speech therapist. You need someone who can really elicit Schuyler's speech," the director said.

"Can we see someone on staff here?" I asked.

Most of the department staff were graduate students who were still learning, she said, and what Schuyler needed was a seasoned professional in private practice who had years of experience with children like Schuyler.

I didn't know any speech therapists, so I asked the director if she could give me some recommendations for local therapists. Thankfully, the first one I called ultimately became Schuyler's speech therapist.

At first, our appointments were twice a week, at $120 per session. That added up to nearly $1,000 per month to help Schuyler talk. The expense was stunning but how could we not do it? How many other families did this? Numerous ones, it turns out. The other parents I met (and let's be honest, ninety-eight percent of the time, it was the mom) in the waiting rooms of various clinicians became my first layer of support. I asked the mom how she'd heard about the therapist, how long they had been going, how it was working, and other questions I was hungry to have answered. Hey, maybe we could get our respective gangs together some time! Were we in the same school district? What other advice might she have for me? I was starving for connections and information, and other moms seemed to be the only source.

When I recall the first few years of seeking diagnosis and treatment for Schuyler, I remember having only one person ever ask *me* how *I* was. Schuyler was always the focus of an appointment, routine or preliminary, and I understand that, but I was feeling the brunt of this, too. Some practitioners treated me like Schuyler's taxi service and didn't acknowledge me as they walked over to the waiting area to call us back to their office. Had someone actually taken the time to ask genuinely, "And so, Mrs. Walker, how are you?" I might have answered, "Falling apart, thank you. You?"

I vividly remember sitting in our pediatrician's office on two separate visits with Schuyler, sobbing about how daily life was so freaking hard, amid the havoc Schuyler had caused in the exam room while we were waiting . . . and waiting. The entire time the pediatrician was in the room with us, he never asked why I was so upset. He never offered any compassion, comfort, or indication that he knew that all was not well in my world. I would have settled for him motioning to the box of Kleenex on his desk or offering a "Motherhood and You" pamphlet. Nothing. Despite doing everything I had been told to do by the people who knew what to do, I was no closer to greater insight about Schuyler than before I hopped on this hamster wheel of pain. All I had to show for the months of chasing answers were fewer dollars in the bank, lost hours of sleep, and a fond appreciation of the low cost of some decent hospital cafeterias.

The speech therapy appointments were not as I expected. The first few sessions were like expensive ice cream socials, minus the ice cream, all getting-to-know-you vibes. Our therapist, though, was awesome. With three boys of her own, I quickly felt she was capable of reaching Schuyler and helping in a way that we could not. Each session was fifty minutes long. Most appointments, I would stay and observe, knowing that I needed to learn how to work with Schuyler when she wasn't there; other times, I had just enough time to haul Connor in his car seat down the block to Panera for an iced tea and a few seconds of peace. Returning to pick up Schuyler, I would chat with the therapist for a few minutes about his progress, tips for home, etc. That feedback and information was great, but they never seemed like enough.

It occurred to me that what I really needed was a speech therapist in my house, working with Schuyler from sunrise to sunset. No matter how good the therapist was, there was no way that Schuyler was going to learn to speak by being dropped off two times a week for nearly an hour. So we discontinued his speech therapy, and using the tools that I had picked up while sitting in on Schuyler's sessions, I added the job as Schuyler's speech therapist to my growing to-do list.

From the moment that Schuyler first woke up, standing in his crib and cooing for me to come into his bedroom, I made it my personal mission to pull every word out his mouth that I could. Every time he pointed and grunted at something, I would say its name. "Book? Book? BUH-OOK. Book." Holding the book in my hand, getting closer to him, I kept repeating, "BOOK." I imagined a rope with my hands on one end and Schuyler's mouth on the other, and I constantly pulled to get those words I knew were in there OUT! My voice was often hoarse at the end of the day, and by evening, I had to remind myself to keep offering him the words he needed instead of just handing the book to him.

Ironically, Schuyler's first word was "Daddy." On Mother's Day. "DAAD-dee!" he chortled. It melted me to hear his voice, and I anticipated a flurry of words to follow, but instead, he only said a handful of words: *truck, train, no.* He was still unable to make sentences, and his frustration and meltdowns continued as I kept engaging him to get him to talk.

The decision to discontinue Schuyler's original speech therapy sessions after two months was a good one. It didn't help that midway through, I had discovered that our insurance company would not cover any of the sessions. That meant that we had to pay about $2,000 out of pocket. It had been six months since I left my corporate job that provided health insurance for our family and had since transferred coverage to Dave's employer, which offered a different benefit package. Turns out it does make a difference which insurance carrier you have, although that alone would not have covered our sessions.

In the letter denying coverage of our sessions, the

insurer stated that since Schuyler had never spoken, there was no speech to regain, so there was no need for speech therapy. Oh, really? So why was it that my grandfather, who had been diagnosed with Alzheimer's disease, was receiving speech therapy that was covered? Where was the logic in paying for speech therapy for the grandfather, yet denying speech therapy for the grandson? Why focus spending on end-of-life treatment rather than investing in beginning-of-life treatment? Before dementia consumed his life, my grandfather had over eighty amazing years—he raised five girls, built businesses, served his country, traveled the world, invented products, and enjoyed life. Schuyler had never had an amazing year.

This experience got me to thinking about returning to my first love, public policy. If I was coming up against this obstacle, other families were as well. In my opinion, that was a flawed policy. I thought, *I know how a bill becomes a law*, and later that afternoon, I picked up the phone to talk with our state representative. Thankfully, she was available and took a few moments out of her day to listen. These kinds of policies, I argued, have legislative solutions. "Please tell me how I can help you get this done," I pleaded. I didn't know it then, but that brief experience would plunge me back into the deep end of legislative advocacy, trips to D.C., and graduate school for a master's degree in public policy and administration.

Another suggestion that came from the speech and language evaluation was to pursue an occupational therapy evaluation. *What do you mean, occupational?* I wondered. *Schuyler doesn't have a job. His occupation is being a kid!* Some professionals suggested some of Schuyler's issues were caused by a lack of awareness of where his body was in relation to the space around him, or perhaps he had a problem with his balance or some other motor or sensory impairment. They threw around terms like proprioception, vestibular, and apraxic. Come again? Was that even English? It was like being in a foreign country without a translator. And although these experts had a lot of theories, they had no answers. Some practitioners were not parents and simply could not relate to what life in our house looked like.

As I tried to provide Schuyler with the help he needed at home, I got some guidance from an unexpected source. When Schuyler had attended the preschool church program, one good thing happened, though at first it was in disguise. During his first days there, the teachers asked that I stay nearby in case Schuyler needed me as he made the adjustment, so I spent a precious three-hour period each preschool day stuck in the church library, rocking, nursing, and playing with Connor. One day, as Connor slept in the stroller, I came across a book in one of the tall stacks. It was entitled *Late-Talking Children*, written by Thomas Sowell. A father with a child who was very bright but struggled to talk, Sowell found that there were other children like his son. Like Schuyler. I pushed the stroller over to a table and sat down with the book in my hand. Eagerly, I thumbed through it.

In his book, Sowell describes his son and other children who didn't talk at two or three or even four years of age. But these children—many of them boys—exhibited normal to above-average intelligence and were good at music, math, and memory. That was certainly Schuyler. Dave has a background in civil engineering, and both my grandfather and great-grandfather were engineers.

Maybe, Sowell suggests, these kids' analytical abilities develop first, and their speech develops later. Unfortunately, Sowell said, some late-talking children are thought to be autistic or to have cognitive deficiencies and are placed in special education classes without digging further into their abilities.

I thought about that book later that morning when I picked up Schuyler, as I watched him play with his cars, rolling them back and forth on the preschool's hardwood floor. Like the kids in Sowell's book, Schuyler understood me. He knew what was going on around him. Could the answer be that simple, that one area of his brain was developing ahead of the part of his brain that affected speech? I was so excited to realize that there might be other people who struggled with a late talker, too. What were their stories? What insights might they offer? That afternoon, as soon as the kids were down for naps, my hand was on the phone, tracking down Thomas Sowell. With surprisingly few phone calls, I reached him at his office at Stanford University.

"Hi—I'm Christine Walker, and my son, Schuyler is a late talker," I blurted when he answered the phone. "I'm so sorry to bother you, but I'm just so desperate for answers. Do you have a few minutes to talk with me?" I don't know whether he could hear the anxiety in my voice, but he was perfectly lovely and patient.

"Of course, Christine," he said. "How can I help you?"

In that moment, Thomas Sowell was heaven sent! I told him that the specialists said I shouldn't worry because boys talk later, but I didn't know how late was late. They also said that Schuyler needed speech therapy and occupational therapy, and I couldn't afford both.

"Christine, I understand—I've been just where you are," he said. "It sounds like you need to get in touch with the right expert. I know the professor at Vanderbilt University who runs the speech and language department. His name is Stephen Camarata. He may be able to help you figure out what steps to take."

"Thank you so much," I said gratefully, and then prepared for my next phone call.

"Hi, Dr. Camarata," I began. "This is Christine Walker, a mom desperately searching for answers for her son. Thomas Sowell suggested that I contact you. Would you mind if I asked you a few questions?"

"Christine, how can I help?" Dr. Camarata replied, with a smile in his voice.

"It's my son, Schuyler. He doesn't talk yet, and we've been going from one expert to another, and I have a legal pad full of nine different things I was told to do by therapists, clinicians, and doctors, and I can't do all of these!" I could feel my voice get tighter and tighter and my breath come faster as I staved off hysteria. How could I help my son when I couldn't afford, or get to, all of the treatment everyone was telling me he needed? Even if I could, there was simply not enough time in the day to do everything that was recommended. And to make matters worse, nothing we had tried so far had made a dent.

"Dr. Camarata," I said, "all of this is new to me. Can you please help me prioritize?" I waited, again hanging onto every word he had to offer.

"Tell me what types of therapies have been recommended," he said calmly, and I gave him the rundown off my scribbled-over yellow legal pad.

"Well, in all honesty, occupational therapy is not going

to get your son to talk," he said. And just that simply, it made perfect sense. Those few minutes with Dr. Camarata brought clarity I had not had in nearly a year. Schuyler's problem was more speech than sensory, and it always had been. Although he was sensitive to sensory stimuli like loud noises and certain textures, his inability to speak had always seemed to be at the root of his behavior.

"Thank you so much," I said, looking at my watch and realizing we had talked for half an hour. Dr. Camarata had helped me focus on the greatest area of need: speech.

This—working with Schuyler at home, hunting down experts like an obsessed detective—continued month after month for over a year, with me popping Excedrin Quick Tabs like they were breath mints, until the grunting and pointing method subsided and Schuyler, at last, began to speak. I loved the sweet sound of his little boy voice as words began to replace grunts and pointing. "Mom," he said one day, and my heart melted. But my happiness at his increasing ability to express himself was tempered by his frustration level still being high, despite his access to speech.

Both Thomas Sowell and Steven Camarata had provided me with expert insights that helped me understand Schuyler's needs better. But during this time (and many times throughout our journey), I also found that the expert doesn't always know best.

I checked in with Schuyler's pediatrician to let him know what progress we had—or had not—made, and he suggested I have Schuyler evaluated by yet another expert, an internationally known psychiatrist who was regarded throughout the medical community as "The Guy" to see for all things autism. This clinician had mentored many other doctors and served on several task forces, including one created by the governor.

Of course, I knew about autism. I had seen the movie *Rain Man*. I knew that it involved repetitive behavior, a lack of eye contact, and not wanting to be touched. That didn't describe Schuyler at all! Schuyler loved to snuggle and cuddle. He loved to laugh and interact . . . on his good days, at least. But we still lacked the key to Schuyler's behavior issues, so I decided to follow our pediatrician's advice anyway and called The Guy to make an appointment for a neuro-psych evaluation.

"Certainly, Mrs. Walker," said the receptionist politely. "The doctor's next available appointment is in . . . eight months. Shall I book that for you?"

Eight months? She had to be kidding me. I was not waiting eight freaking months to find out what this was or how to make it better. Once again, I took to the phones to figure out who else could see Schuyler. Thankfully, I was able to get an appointment with another doctor within the month and looked forward to maybe, just maybe, making some progress.

I got my chance to see The Guy about a year later, when he spoke at a local high school about autism. Although I might not get personal attention from him, I was anxious to hear what he had to say. Sensory issues are among the first clues that autism might be knocking on your child's door, and while lack of speech, tantrums, difficulty transitioning, and uncontrolled giddiness were some of Schuyler's behaviors, he was also extremely sensitive to noises, materials, and clothing. While you or I might hear a plane flying nearby and barely notice,

Schuyler felt the vibrations reverberate through his body as if a 747 were hovered overhead. He wanted to wear sunglasses even on cloudy days. I had to cut the tags out of most of his clothes so that flap of material wouldn't constantly bother him. He hated certain textures, fabrics, and parts of clothing. To this day, Schuyler cannot stand wearing pants that do not have elastic waistbands, often wears his underwear inside out to avoid feeling the tag on the band, and will not put on a polo shirt because of the flap of fabric on the inside of the shirt, which rubs against his chest. Food textures, such as mushy bananas, and smells, such as fragrant sauces, were also a challenge. Schuyler still couldn't stand to walk in grass or sand. And if he came across a feeling or sound he couldn't handle, he'd lose it, crying, screaming, falling to the ground, and flailing his limbs. It didn't matter where we were—the park, the yard, or inside the house—his tantrums were the same. Maybe The Guy could at least help me understand how we could help Schuyler with this.

The school auditorium was full and abuzz when I walked in. I excused myself as I squeezed past the legs of other anxious parents already seated. Most, if not all, of us were haggard, exhausted moms, looking like crap after yet another day of being us. It was more than clear that none of us would be gracing the cover of a fashion magazine any time soon.

As the program was winding down, The Guy took questions from the packed audience. A woman seated in front of me waved her hand frantically to get his attention.

"My son has sensory integration dysfunction," she began, speaking loudly to be heard throughout the room. "It's just so hard to take him anywhere because we never know what he'll react to. What do you suggest, Doctor?" Hundreds of heads bobbed in unison at the mom's question, as that was our daily existence, too. The Guy paused for a moment.

"You will not like my answer," he began. "I don't believe that disorder exists."

A collective gasp echoed through the room. I shook my head in disbelief. Really? Sensory integration or processing disorder did NOT exist? *Come to my house, pal*, I thought, *and watch my son drop to the floor screaming because he can't stand some surface he's touching. Look at how he has to wear sunglasses when he is inside and near a window, or look at how he vomits at the smell of food he doesn't like, and then tell me sensory integration dysfunction doesn't exist.* I wanted to stand up and shout at The Guy and rip him a new one, telling him that he didn't know what he was talking about. And then I realized: he didn't know what *I* was talking about. He had no idea what I was experiencing, or what was going on in my family, or in any of the families of the desperate moms around me. He was an expert in his own right, sure, but he wasn't an expert on *my* life or *my* son. Although The Guy's presentation didn't give me the information I was hoping to find, it provided a valuable insight that "experts" don't have all the answers. This has proven to be true in many other cases.

From that night on, I have stood firm in my belief that the letters after a professional's name paled in comparison to the letters after mine: M.O.M.

...

December 2004. It had been two years since we started down this road to find out what was going on with

Schuyler. I sat outside the child and adolescent psychiatrist's door—the one Schuyler had seen instead of The Guy—and waited to be called into the office. She had seen Schuyler twice and now was ready to make a diagnosis. An answer, finally. Maybe it was some kind of hormone imbalance that the right prescription would remedy. His speech had improved, particularly in the last year, and although he was able to communicate at will, his frustration levels remained inconsistently high. I sighed. To be honest, I didn't know what to expect.

"Mrs. Walker?" The receptionist motioned for me. I followed her into the doctor's office and sat stiffly in a chair in front of her desk. As I waited for the doctor, I wondered what was going on at home. Deciding to divide and conquer, I had gone to the doctor's appointment with Schuyler while Dave stayed home with Connor and now Sloane, our nine-month-old baby girl.

"Hello, Mrs. Walker," the doctor said as she walked into the room. She shook my hand and sat down at her desk. She set down the folder she had carried in and looked at me for a moment. Schuyler was with us in the room, and my attention was divided between keeping him from dismantling her filing cabinet or throwing her paperweights against the wall and listening to what she was saying.

"So," she started, "I've seen Schuyler twice and had him take numerous tests to determine what may be causing his behaviors. You have also provided a really comprehensive family history."

Minus Dave's side, I silently added.

"You've also given me a good portrait of daily life at home," she continued. "That has given me a 360-degree view of Schuyler."

I nodded eagerly.

"Based on these results, I believe that Schuyler has autism, attention deficit hyperactivity disorder—or ADHD—and bipolar disorder," she said carefully.

"Really?" I said faintly.

My heart thumped in my chest, with an accompanying throb in my head. Was she serious? I mean, she wouldn't joke about this, but how could this be? Autism? Maybe he did have ADHD, but bipolar? My God! In five minutes, we had tumbled down the rabbit hole from quasi-manageable behavior issues to mental illness.

My understanding of mental illness was limited at the time, but what I did know made me cringe. Didn't people with bipolar disorder have lives filled with horrid challenges? Weren't most homeless people mentally ill? What the hell would Schuyler's teenage years look like? The memory of the tragedy at Columbine High School swept over me. I felt the blood run from my head, and my arms weakened. This was not just about Schuyler. This level of illness would impact our entire family, including our younger children, who were then two years old and nine months old. Safety was a concern. Chaos, disruption, and screaming were constants. Holding Sloane, my infant daughter, while at the same time keeping Schuyler from trying to hit, kick, or bite Connor was a full-time effort. Just trying to get through a day, not to mention paying bills, all made meeting Schuyler's needs truly challenging. Many days had brought me to my knees, consumed with defeat and discouragement. Learning what was really going on with Schuyler meant that since this was for the rest of his life, it was going to be for the rest of mine. My unwavering quest for answers had led me to this moment. But now it felt as though the psychiatrist had dumped a sack full of gym weights in my lap. I couldn't move.

The doctor stopped talking as she noticed me staring blankly at her, thoughts racing, unshed tears in my eyes. She began drawing pictures of the brain: what each part controls and regulates. She added descriptions of what synapses are, how neurotransmitters work, and how medication can aid in the process of making this well-oiled machine hum as designed. "What other questions do you have?" she paused to ask.

I had a bunch, but the one foremost on my mind was: "What medication should we start with?" I eyed her prescription pad. I would not leave her office without something to take to the pharmacy and give Schuyler that day. Now that we knew the cause, the relief could not come soon enough.

> *"Optimism is the faith that leads to achievement.*
> *Nothing can be done without hope and confidence."*
> —Helen Keller

"To live without hope is to cease to live."
—Fyodor Dostoevsky

CHAPTER 3
SEARCH FOR A CURE

Nearly every day of the past two years had been filled with chaos, screams, tears, grunts, and uncontrollable, sometimes dangerous, behavior. Sure, having three children under the age of four could bring any mom to her knees, but it was much more than that. At several points during each day, I would gulp down a few pain pills to keep a migraine at bay. On a super tough day, I would dig into a prescription medicine I had kept from a previous back injury. I'd take half a pill to help me get through the day, but I didn't want to risk becoming addicted, so I eventually went to my primary care physician, who prescribed an anti-depressant. While these medications helped, exhaustion and frustration were still the norm, as was exasperation. And there was rarely any relief during Schuyler's waking hours.

On the rare "on" days, Schuyler knew not to come into my room and wake me up. He would walk by the doorway, see that I was sleeping, and either go back into his room to play or head downstairs to eat the snack I'd left for him and watch the train video we'd left in the TV the night before. On his typical "off" days, he stood by my bed and shook me or yelled to wake me up. He could not be redirected to another activity and would run into Connor and Sloane's room to wrench them from sleep as well. "Sky, you can't do that," I'd reprimand him. "But I need to do that," he replied. Not want, but need. It was constant bedeviling, emptying the linen closet, taking out all the cereal from the pantry and throwing the boxes on the floor . . . I was still nursing Sloane and often could not jump up to intervene. All I could do was clean up the messes. All three children were in diapers.

We had tried everything seen and unseen to stabilize Schuyler's mood and behavior. We tried gluten-free diets, casein-free diets, vitamins, horseback riding therapy, more vitamins, speech therapy, occupational therapy, neurofeedback, new vitamins, family therapy . . . You name it, and we tried it. Every time I heard about an approach another family tried that worked, we hopped on that bandwagon, hoping for positive results of our own. But to no avail. We were way beyond the sticker chart phase and had yet to tackle the greatest challenge, which was to smooth out Schuyler's behavior. He was miserable. We were miserable.

Some mornings, I hated waking up. I would open my eyes and listen to the chaos that awaited me on an off day. Schuyler was usually up and delighting in destroying whatever he could, whether it was throwing folded laundry into the air or toy cars against the wall and window, his laugh getting louder and more excited as he surveyed the results of his work. His laugh, so different from the light giggles of the young twin toddlers who lived next door, only reminded me that I was in for another day of being me. My life was the movie *Groundhog Day* stuck in a repeat cycle. Something had to shift. Something had to change. Something had to make things less awful—for all of us. And that thing might very well be sitting in a medicine vial on the kitchen windowsill.

After two years of questions to find out what was wrong, I was ready to find solutions. But Dave wasn't so sure we had the right diagnosis yet. Quickly, this became a standoff. Because I was with Schuyler all day and saw his very changeable behavior, I was ready to do whatever it took to help him regulate his behavior, including medicine. Dave, who was at home less often, did not see that behavior up close and personal like I did and perhaps thought my descriptions were simply those of an overwhelmed mother of three children under four years old. At the doctor's office, I had been itching for a prescription that would help Schuyler, but once I filled it, I held off on giving it to him for a few days, wavering in the momentousness of this decision. Finally, though, I had had enough. I knew I shouldn't make this decision unilaterally, but Dave was out of town. As I heard Schuyler throwing toys and books against the wall of his room, I picked up the phone.

Dave was flying back home from New York after visiting a client, but six hours suddenly felt like too long to wait to sit down, have a calm conversation, and make a joint decision. I simply could not wait another second to get some relief into Schuyler's system. I had to let Dave know I was giving Schuyler his first dose of Risperdal. *Now.*

Dave was sitting on the tarmac at LaGuardia when I called. I hated having tough conversations with him over the phone; we had better conversations in person, or at least I thought we did. I felt I was heard better, could explain better, and could more easily read emotions and nuances. But this conversation could not wait, despite the controversial topic. Dave was far more reluctant than I was to give Schuyler medication. He said he was worried about the damage the meds might do, but I think his reluctance had more to do with a resistance to facing the truth. "Yes, he's a little overly active," Dave would acknowledge.

"He is not a little hyperactive, Dave," I would say, exasperated. "Two separate pre-schools have asked us to leave. Some days are filled with complete and total devastation. This is a lot more than a little ADHD."

As a couple, both Dave and I had certain non-negotiables going into our marriage. It was essential to Dave that each of our kids was baptized Catholic, for example. Done. This was mine: if it might help him, Schuyler was going to take medication as part of his broader treatment plan. To withhold medication was ridiculous to me. If Schuyler had diabetes, would it make sense to refuse giving him insulin? If Schuyler had broken his leg, would we not let the ER doctor put a cast on him? Why was this treatment any different? In my mind, it wasn't.

"Hi, honey, it's me," I said when Dave picked up the call.

"Hey, what's up?" Dave responded lightly.

"Listen I know that this isn't the perfect time to talk about this, but the doctor prescribed medication for Schuyler, and I want to give him the first dose." I paused, already steeling myself for his response, before adding, "I know that you don't want to do this, and I respect that. But you have deal breakers, and so do I, and this is one of them."

There was a long silence as I stood in the upstairs bathroom, holding my cell phone in one hand and the prescription bottle in the other.

Then Dave said, "Okay, but if anything bad happens, it's your fault."

In retrospect, I can only imagine how Dave was feeling, buckled into his seat on the plane, passengers on either side, while we talked about this. Dave loved Schuyler, no doubt, but I don't think he truly understood the breadth and depth of what Schuyler and I had been going through. I don't think he accepted or wanted to accept that his child had a mental illness. To give Schuyler medicine for bipolar disorder was to actually acknowledge that Schuyler *had* bipolar disorder.

Still, when Dave told me that I was to blame if anything happened to Schuyler after taking the medicine, my heart hurt. Hearing that filled me with the first wave of solitude that would become my constant companion in the coming years. I realized I would be going it alone. And I was willing to do that, if it meant finding something, anything, that would help Schuyler. But it surprised me as well; Dave was such an incredible dad! From being in the delivery room and holding Schuyler even before I did, to going to the grocery store at ten o'clock at night if we were out of diapers and milk, Dave loved being a father. On the day we met, both of us talked about how much we wanted to be parents. It never occurred to me that we would not see eye to eye on issues concerning any of our children's health.

Risperdal wafers were our first entry into the world of pharmacology. I didn't take chemistry in high school and ran away from as many science classes as I could, but this experiment forced me to become an expert in organic chemistry, neuroscience, genetics, brain development, and molecular biology nearly overnight. I had more questions for our psychiatrist than a session would allow answers. I scoured library shelves, bugged research librarians, and surfed online for any information that would help my unscientific brain grasp Schuyler's condition and, more importantly, how exactly medication interacted with neurotransmitters. One question I neglected to ask our doctor, though, was, "How do we know what medication will work best?"

The good news about medication for brain disorders is that there are dozens of options available to patients. The bad news about medication for brain disorders is that there are dozens of options available to patients. Ugh! Begin spinning the pharmacological roulette wheel! Nailing down the precise medication, correct dosage, ideal time of day to take the meds, and, in the case of certain conditions such as bipolar disorder, what combination of medications will offer the greatest relief of symptoms was the single most challenging piece of this puzzle.

Many psychiatrists will tell you that in about a decade, we will have many more tools at our disposal to diagnose, treat, and manage brain disorders. That's great. But what do we do today? There is no blood test to determine a diagnosis. There is no MRI or functional MRI to identify a brain disorder. An official diagnosis can be made only by a child and adolescent psychiatrist, which doesn't seem like much of a problem, until you learn that there is a huge shortage of child and adolescent psychiatrists across the country. According to the American Academy of Child and Adolescent Psychiatry, there are only roughly 8,000 practitioners today. (I once spoke with a woman from Wyoming who confirmed that there were only three child and adolescent psychiatrists in her entire state. Many families had to travel to Salt Lake City or Denver for treatment.) Nearly 30,000 are needed to meet current demand, not to mention the anticipated future demand. In addition, many private practices either are not accepting new patients or do not accept private insurance, and for families with Medicaid, the scarcity of practitioners in their area that have agreed to serve these children means they often must wait for months to be seen.

All of this makes for a very, very difficult search for answers. I say *answers* because today, there is no cure for autism or mental illness. Yet. So what do I do in the meantime? Whatever works.

Our search for answers was fraught with minuscule victories and soul-crushing setbacks. It took fifteen months and nine different medications (mood stabilizers, SSRIs, anti-seizure medications) to find one that worked for Schuyler. In the course of those fifteen months, Schuyler experienced negative side effects from various regimens. The Risperdal we tried first increased his appetite, and he packed on about ten pounds. Seroquel caused Schuyler to sleep all the time, and he looked stoned when he was awake. Depakote took some of the edge off Schuyler's mood, but when we added Lithium, his naturally lush, thick hair became thin and wiry and began collecting in the bathtub drain. Other meds seemed to have no effect, while increasing, decreasing, or combining meds often showed results, but not lasting ones. We tried wafers, pills, skin patches, and even powder forms of medication delivery, all with mixed success. The skin patches caused rashes, some pills were too big for Schuyler to swallow, and powder mixed into milk or juice made it hard for him to finish the whole glass.

During this time, I learned that for many parents, finding the right medicine is a result of trial and error. Both Dave and I were frustrated because we didn't know what to expect, and with each negative side effect, Dave would say, "See? This is why I didn't want to give him this!" I didn't have an answer, either, but I had to keep trying something.

I began keeping detailed notes on what each medicine was doing. After the amount of time I was told it would take to work, I would report the results to the doctor and we would decide whether to continue that medicine, change the dosage, or add another medicine to help the first one work better. Once, I called a well-known child psychiatrist in Pittsburgh after reading about a paper he had published on the side effects of using lithium and Depakote together. When I told the doctor that Schuyler was experiencing hair loss, he simply asked if the combination was effective. That was a huge moment for me, as the truth was that it was *not* working. I realized that these were the times I needed to lead the team and not rely on conventional wisdom. I called Schuyler's doctor and said I wanted to discontinue the lithium, as he'd been on Depakote before without any hair loss. She agreed, so we introduced a different medication: Geodon.

Geodon was our godsend. Two days after he started taking it, Schuyler was calmer, focused, and far less irritable. His doctor was thrilled with the result and added that many people have luck on Geodon.

"Why didn't we just start with Geodon then?" I asked over the phone, exasperated.

Patiently, she replied, "There was no way of knowing what would work until we tried it."

This experience fuels much of the work I now do, pushing corporations and public agencies to work toward creating a blood test that can tell a doctor what disorder a patient has, detailing the chemical balance and metabolism to shed some light on what med has the best chance of working on one's particular mental health concern. No parent should have to watch his or her child suffer on the necessary-evil path of finding the right treatment. I was just grateful that we finally seemed to have found something that worked.

Silly me for thinking our quest was over.

"Hope is the thing with feathers that perches in the soul and sings the tune without the words and never stops at all."
—Emily Dickinson

"Hope smiles from the threshold of the year to come, whispering 'it will be happier.'"
—Alfred Lord Tennyson

CHAPTER 4
NO ANSWERS IN SIGHT

Before I married and became a parent, I always imagined that whenever a child became sick, the parents would band together, keeping a constant bedside vigil, praying for their child to get well. Long after the parents left the hospital, friends, family, classmates, and neighbors would rally around in their time of need, dropping off food, running errands, organizing fundraisers, doing everything they could to bring some joy or relief to someone they cared about. So imagine my surprise, dismay, and disbelief, at finding that there were no warm faces lining up outside our front door, ready to lift our weary souls as we worked to get Schuyler well.

Schuyler's diagnosis wasn't the kind that would allow me to tell my neighbors and rally the troops to get our family through this. Other families in our town had children with cancer and were completely enveloped in love and support. They could count on a parade of casseroles, offers of driving kids to and from soccer practice, free house cleaning, yard signs praying for recovery, fundraisers, sponsored trips to Hawaii, support groups for spouses and siblings, and an abundance of empathy.

I wouldn't wish cancer on anyone, least of all my child, but mental illness still carries with it a stigma and that keeps most people and support resources at bay. Unlike children (and adults for that matter) with visible challenges, such as Down syndrome or cerebral palsy, children (and again, adults for that matter) with emotional or behavioral challenges can repel those around them. There is no "he brings out the best in everyone he meets" comment about boys like Schuyler. We don't get many invitations to birthday parties. The social skills group we joined in an effort to enhance Schuyler's ability to be successful around others disbanded once the parents learned that Schuyler was in it.

My exhaustion at chasing answers to make Schuyler well was matched only by depression. I felt like an island, an island so remote the Coast Guard didn't have it on any map. It just wasn't fair. Why was Schuyler's illness different from other kids' illnesses?

A good friend of mine, Natalie, who has a son profoundly affected by autism, once lamented that a family that lived in her neighborhood went on an all-expenses paid trip to Maui, courtesy of Make-A-Wish foundation. The family's daughter had successfully completed treatment for a brain tumor, and the trip was a welcome respite. "Where's MY trip to Maui?" Natalie shouted, adding that her son's "brain tumor" would never go away. In no way was Natalie dismissing the trauma of having a severely ill child. What she was getting at was what so many families raising children with autism or mental illness experience, which is a lack of empathy and support. Natalie struck a chord that millions of families throughout the country feel every day.

For years, I felt as though I could not ask for any help from neighbors, as Schuyler did not look sick; he only behaved differently. He behaved worse, according to many. Neighbors would scoop up their young kids who were playing on their front lawn to make sure "that Walker kid" would not come over and make trouble. I couldn't blame them. It was not unusual for Schuyler to push a child off his or her own swing set or Big Wheel so he could have a turn. When Schuyler was upset at having to wait to play with the backhoe in the sandbox at the park, he would throw sand around the entire area in protest. One neighbor said she couldn't have her kids see Schuyler's behavior, as her kids "might think acting like that is okay." Another time, we joined a local social skills group that had only two other kids. We only met once a week, and the goal was to help Schuyler with the ins and outs of playing with kids his age in a safe and appropriate way. Essentially, it was a play date with wingmen. The night before the second scheduled session, the director of the center called me to say that the other parents (all two of them) had called her to say that they were pulling out of the group. Maybe they had heard me talking to the receptionist about Schuyler's behavior, or maybe one of the kids told a parent something Schuyler had said to him. In any case, like many other families we had encountered up to that point, they withdrew. The director apologized for delivering news she knew was tough for me to hear. She didn't offer any explanation, nor did she offer any other options at the center, and I didn't have it in me to ask about a different program that we might be asked to leave again.

The collective effect of social abandonment was to

retreat into our house. It felt as though we were living in a bunker, a separate universe that had little contact with the outside world, save for saying hello and thank you to our mail carrier. It was just too hard. Too many questions about Schuyler's behavior when we ventured outside, too much explaining, too much apologizing, too much rejection. And with two younger kids in tow wherever we went, it was simply too tough. No friends, no playgroups, no preschools. The days were dark and mercilessly long. I was desperate to talk with another woman in my situation. If I could only find one.

In late fall of 2004, we moved to Winnetka and, as newcomers, got a visit from the Welcome Wagon lady. She came with a basket of information on the town and its activities. I was so glad to have a few minutes to chat with a live adult that we stood in my front yard and began talking like old friends while Schuyler ran around.

"Your son is very busy," she said, noting Schuyler's almost frantic dashing back and forth. An understatement.

I shrugged. "He has a lot of energy."

"I used to teach kindergarten in the school district for many years," she said. "I just do this to make sure I get out of the house. But I've seen a few children like your little one before." She paused and looked at me. "Have you ever had him assessed for autism?"

Before I could answer, she put a hand on my arm. "I just wanted to make sure you know that our school district has some wonderful special education programs for children, and if you think it may help, you should contact them."

Those kind, thoughtful words helped introduce me into the lifesaving world of special ed. I enrolled Schuyler in an early childhood program that was part of our local special education district. It was only in the afternoons, but it was the first of many amazing experiences with special education teachers, staff, clinicians, and bus drivers. One of the best days of that year for me was the day the shuttle bus came to pick up Schuyler for his first day of school. When I saw other boys on the bus I thought, *Those boys have* MOTHERS! That meant there were other mothers with boys like Schuyler! I must meet these women!

HIPPA (the Health Insurance Portability and Accountability Act, which guards privacy on health issues) turned out to be a huge hurdle, as neither the bus driver nor teaching staff could tell me who any of these boys were, where they lived, or who their parents were. So it was on to Plan B. I wrote notes to the moms of the boys on the bus and begged the driver to give it to them when the boys got off the bus. The note was a tad cryptic: "Hi, I'm a mom of one of the boys in your son's class who also rides the bus; my son's stop is before yours. I would love to talk with you—can we grab coffee soon?" Including my phone number and email address, I held my breath, hoping that I could find a lifeline in one of the other moms of a son with Schuyler's challenges. No one else seemed to get it or understand what we went through. But I had no luck. I didn't get a single call or email. On to Plan C.

I volunteered to help with the Valentine's Day party in Schuyler's classroom with the sole mission (not that I didn't want to down my weight in those little conversation hearts) of making eye contact with another mom in that room. Success! Finally, I had a chance to find a comrade in the foxhole! I was able to connect with

Carolyn, mom of Teddy, who lived a few minutes up the road from us. I swear Carolyn was as psyched to meet me as I was to meet her. I don't know why she hadn't responded to my "bus" invitation, but if she was mired in the same chaos as I often was, she may not have been up for responding to one more thing. After that, we kept in contact, had our boys over to each other's houses, and tried our best to be there for each other in a way that none of our other friends or family could, or even knew how to be—like understanding when a child had a meltdown or refused to share a toy or didn't want to join in a game, or knowing what a bad day really looked like and encouraging each other through it. It was a small victory.

My circle of support grew the following school year, when Schuyler started kindergarten at a phenomenal therapeutic day school called North Shore Academy (NSA). As part of the special education program in our school district, once Schuyler was identified as needing special ed, he was automatically admitted into this school. This was such an incredible experience that from that first week, I have been a die-hard devotee of therapeutic schools for children who struggle with emotional distress. When I first toured the school, I was struck by the warmth of the staff, the intimate size of the classes, and the positive vibe that pervaded the school.

Therapeutic schools, both day and residential programs, are, in my opinion, one of the greatest gifts to a family raising a child with mental illness. Most of the teachers have advanced degrees in reaching children with challenges in a way that many general education teachers do not. North Shore Academy, for example, was designed to meet the individual needs of kids with autism, anxiety, or mood disorders or other learning or emotional challenges. Every classroom had a handful of students, with a staff-to-student ratio of roughly one to four. The classrooms were designed to reduce or manage common behavior triggers with muted lighting, soundproof walls, sensory equipment, etc. Every task was broken down into manageable chunks. The educational plan was comprehensive and included wraparound services such as social work, occupational therapy, speech and language pathology, group and individual therapy, and an environment that permeated every inch of the school campus. The staff was not restricted by a bell curve when it came to making accommodations for children with challenges. These schools are one of the only places a parent will hear how great their kids are.

North Shore Academy was exactly like that. NSA's approach was better able to meet Schuyler's needs because that was all it did. It was as different from public school as a children's hospital is from a general community hospital; both have medical personnel, but one facility serves one population only, every day, with specialists who possess knowledge, experience, and a willingness to work exclusively with that population and its specific needs. That was NSA. Accommodations were the norm and not the exception. We were home.

I eagerly picked up techniques used at school that I could try at home for Schuyler. The first thing I understood was that Schuyler is a visual learner, which is common for kids who have the challenges that he does. So at school, they had visual reminders of everything. They didn't use words; they used pictures. Kids like Sky can also have a heightened anxiety over what is next, so the teachers would outline the whole day in pictures. Come in, sit down, math, snack—Schuyler could see his whole day at a glance. Then, as each activity was completed, the teachers would remove that picture so that he could get a sense of time passing. It was genius. They would also tell Schuyler what to do instead of what *not* to do. "Schuyler, walk," they would say, instead of "Schuyler, don't run." Through them, I learned not to talk a whole lot. A couple of words were enough for him to process. He could grasp, "Schuyler, shoes now," but he would get lost in, "Schuyler, we are going to the park, so go get your shoes from the closet."

Although school was going gangbusters, home life continued to be a struggle, even with these strategies in place. Most mornings, I would count down the minutes until the cab came to take Schuyler to school. Our cab driver, Boris, was heaven sent. This wonderful older gentleman, who came over to the United States from Russia and had grandchildren of his own, became an important fixture in our family's life. Every day, Boris came bouncing up the stairs to our front porch and greeted us with a hearty "Goot morning," grabbing Schuyler's backpack and guiding him back to the cab for the twenty-minute ride to school. We would see Boris again on the afterschool drop off. On Fridays, Boris would go to McDonald's and get Schuyler his favorite snack of chicken nuggets and French fries. One Friday early on, I made the mistake of attempting to give Boris money as reimbursement for his generosity. Whoops! By his unblinking stare, I realized I had deeply offended him. "It's something I love to do," he said. "It doesn't cost much, and it's a nice way for the boys to start their weekend." Our friendship with

Boris continued for another two years as Schuyler continued at North Shore Academy. To this day, Boris's cell number is in my phone.

The hours that Schuyler was at school were great, as I could then focus on Connor and Sloane, who were four and three by the summer of 2007. Schuyler was usually home by 3:30, which meant that by 3:00, my anxiety rose as I wondered what version of Schuyler would come through the door. If I heard yelling or swearing as he opened the screen door after Boris walked back toward the cab, I knew it was going to be tough the rest of the day and night, and possibly the next morning. When Schuyler was having a particularly bad time, he could be violent toward Connor and Sloane, chasing, hitting, and kicking them, or damage property in the house by punching walls or throwing and breaking objects. When he was no older than five, he started running around saying the "F" word repeatedly. *Where did he get that?* He truly was not himself when the more severe episodes occurred. He would threaten his siblings, saying he wanted to hurt them, which put me on high alert protection mode. Schuyler was always remorseful when he realized what he had done, which would then morph into self-hatred, sending him further into thinking he was a bad person. "I'm stupid," he would lament on occasion, or worse, "I don't deserve to live." He was in such psychic pain himself, and his self-esteem dove with every negative interaction.

What worried me most was when Schuyler went after Connor, who seemed to be the target of Schuyler's aggression. Schuyler had hit him with brooms and toy cars and had bitten him, leaving bruises and other marks.

As time passed, I increasingly worried that someone in our family would be hurt badly. At times, when Schuyler raged out of control, I sent the younger kids to their rooms, assuring them that I would lock their doors from the outside to keep Schuyler out—to keep them safe. I was angry and, at times, bitter. I felt that no one around me understood or could understand. I know this may not have been true, but I imagined that my neighbors' biggest dilemma on any given day was whether they would order cheese or pepperoni pizza for dinner. The other parents I met through the therapeutic day school circuit were a source of strength for me, but few of them had the strife in their home that we had in ours. Who could help me figure this out? I knew that another, deeper level of treatment was needed but didn't really know how to connect the dots. The truth was, I didn't even know what dots existed.

"The true way to soften one's troubles
is to solace those of others."
—Madame De Maintenon

"*We must accept finite disappointment but never lose infinite hope.*"
—Dr. Martin Luther King, Jr.

CHAPTER 5
DECISION POINT

In June 2007, our tired but relaxed family came back home after a short getaway in St. Louis. We didn't take many trips together, so this was a treat. Schuyler behaved well, as did Connor and Sloane, and for a few days, we felt like what I imagined normal families must be like. As soon as we got back home, however, the mood changed. Schuyler started acting like he never had before. He wouldn't sleep. He wouldn't settle down. He wouldn't pay attention to anything I said to him. Even more concerning, he kept trying to hit us, to throw toys and books at us. He could not get himself under control or think through choices. It wasn't just a tantrum or a ploy to get his way. I had never seen Schuyler act this way, and my gut told me this was nothing typical. If I had any doubt, I could recall some of the things he had said, even from the time he was a preschooler.

"I hate you. I'm going to kill you!" Schuyler would say in the middle of a meltdown. And although some children might utter those horrible words in a moment of frustration, when Schuyler said it, I had no doubt that he meant it in that moment. I already knew that, at times, he had difficulty telling the difference between fantasy and reality, so I made sure to be as tuned in as possible whenever I thought Schuyler was waning. Sometimes, he would even recognize it, telling me his brain was going to a "dark place." When Schuyler was very young, most of the mothers I talked to who had older boys with similar challenges would lament how they "couldn't get them out of the basement—all they do is play video games day and night." The second I heard that, I vowed not to have any kind of gaming systems in our home. The image of Schuyler slumped in front of a screen for hours on end, being more a part of a fantasy world than a real one, gave me chills. The very nature of many of the video games in the market repelled me, and I would not allow him to get sucked into some underworld culture of killing as entertainment—and risk not ever getting him back. The same applies to all of my kids: to this day, you will not find an Xbox, PS2, Nintendo DS, or a Wii in our home. (I always say that "We" is more important than "Wii.") While we're not quite *Little House on the Prairie*, I know that the world will soon have more of an influence on my children than I will, and I want them to have a rich foundation of self-reliance, critical thinking, and problem solving before they take that leap.

At the point of Schuyler's bizarre behavior, it had only been two months since the traumatic shooting at Virginia Tech, in which a gunman killed thirty-three people. As is the custom in events of this nature, the media's attention soon turned to "the deranged gunman" and "why he would do such a thing." Before any other information was released, I instinctively knew that the perpetrator was male and had some sort of untreated or undiagnosed mental health issue. My heart sank. I needed to make sure Schuyler never went down that path.

I want to take a moment to reflect on this issue and how it has impacted me, our family, and the collective efforts in legislative advocacy. In the years since that shooting, there have been other horrific events like Virginia Tech, including those in Tucson, Arizona, Aurora, Colorado, and, of course, Newtown, Connecticut. In every case, the perpetrator was indeed a young man with an undiagnosed or untreated mental health issue whose behavior concerned those around him. It is crucial to point out here that each of these men turned to violence as a means of dealing with unresolved issues that had nothing to do with the victims. It concerns me that people often view those living with a mental health concern as violent and unstable. This is simply not the case. Data has proven that those living with a mental health concern are actually more likely to be the victim of a crime than an instigator of it. These high-profile incidents of lethal force inflicted by young men with a mental health concern should be seen as a symptom of the larger problem, which is our badly broken mental health care system. *These cases are examples of the potential consequences of not having access to effective, meaningful, and consistent treatment.* These avoidable tragedies persist for multiple reasons:

- A national shortage of psychiatrists available for evaluation and medication management.
- Insurance plans that do not cover hospital stays long enough to be effective.
- A nearly 90 percent reduction in the number of beds available for those in need of intensive treatment.

- The stigma associated with mental illness that can prevent people from seeking care.
- A lack of available supportive housing.
- State budgets that have eliminated supportive programs.
- Denial of the condition by the family or individual.
- Privacy laws that can prevent schools from sharing medical information with parents.

When seen in this light, it becomes clear that additional work in public policy is needed to correct disparities that have existed for decades.

That weekend, after our return from St. Louis, Schuyler was not sleeping and was constantly screaming in the yard and out the window, and running after Connor, who kept running away from his brother.

"What is going on?" Dave turned to me, rattled, as he picked up Connor and held him up high, while Schuyler kept lunging up, trying to hit Connor.

"I don't know," I said helplessly. Dave had never seen this side of Schuyler, despite my descriptions to him. Even I had never seen Schuyler this dysregulated, this angry and unable to manage his emotions.

Later in the day, I left for my shift at our local children's fair, an annual event that had a giant slide, pony rides, game booths, and a bake sale on the village green. I had agreed to work at the popcorn booth for a few hours and had the last shift of the day. The kids stayed home with Dave, as I knew bringing all three of them (and certainly with Schuyler in the state he was) would have been a bad idea. When I got back home, Dave told me that something had happened while I was gone.

"Schuyler went after Connor while they were all playing in the basement," he said.

"Is everyone okay?" I asked, my heart racing. "Where's Schuyler?"

Our basement had wall-to-wall Thomas trains and wooden track, and Schuyler had grabbed a train and aimed at Connor's head. Dave had reached for Schuyler, but Schuyler broke loose and fell into one of the piles of trains instead, thankfully missing Connor by a few feet.

"Schuyler got a bruise on his face. Other than that, they're fine," Dave reassured me.

I went over to see Schuyler for a close-up look and to make sure he was feeling okay.

"How are you doing, pal?" I asked, tilting his head up to see the red mark on his right cheek.

"I'm okay," he said matter-of-factly. "I fell. Dad put ice on it." He turned and went back to assembling his train track. He was calm, and his cheek, while bruised, wasn't badly swollen. I thought we were out of the woods.

Dave was visibly moved at how badly that afternoon and the previous day had gone. "I just had no idea," he kept saying to me when we were alone. I couldn't help feeling validated: *Yep*, I thought. *Welcome to my life! See, I TOLD you how things were at home when you weren't here!* We found out later that Schuyler's behavior represented his first manic episode and that more would likely follow.

Monday morning, Schuyler's cheek was still tender to the touch and the bruise was a decided purplish-blue. Dave left that morning for a work trip to Los Angeles, and Schuyler's behavior was still very off. He had difficulty sticking with his routine and following directions. It was as if he just couldn't control himself.

Schuyler had school that morning, and I wanted to make sure his teachers were aware of what had happened over the weekend. I liked to let them know whenever he had a particularly challenging evening or weekend so they might be better prepared for his behavior at school. Likewise, I wanted them to let me know when he had a difficult day at school so I might better plan for our evening at home.

"Schuyler was really upset all weekend, and I have never seen him like this," I explained to the school social worker, telling her about Schuyler's episode and bruise. She assured me she would make sure his teachers were aware and that they would keep a close watch on him. I told her that I was in close contact with his doctor and that we were doing our best to keep him, and the other kids, safe and did not feel hospitalization was necessary at that point. In just a few weeks, Schuyler was due to fly to Camp Buckskin in Ely, Minnesota, for a month of good old-fashioned fun, and I suspected the camp would not accept him after an in-patient psychiatric hospital stay. Camp Buckskin is an incredible family owned and operated therapeutic camp for kids who have a variety of brain disorders, including Asperger's, ADHD, mental illness, and others, and while the camp was a great fit for Schuyler, it benefitted me, too: I needed a break from the daily drama and chaos.

Later that morning, the phone rang. It was the school social worker again. This time, instead of the sympathetic tone she used when I talked to her earlier, her voice was cool and official. "Mrs. Walker, I talked it over with the principal and school nurse . . . I called Department of Children and Family Services. I think I'll have them figure out what *really* happened to Schuyler."

A beat passed before I realized what she meant: she thought we had abused Schuyler! How could she possibly think that? In the two years we had been at the school, hadn't we shown what kind of people we were? I had told her what happened! I had called her! Did abusive parents willingly and proactively tell state-mandated reporters? Hit Schuyler? Really? I was livid but had to keep my emotions in check, as Connor and Sloane were still at home, enjoying the peaceful Monday morning respite without their brother.

Dave was en route to Los Angeles and not reachable by phone for another few hours. Why was I handling this inquisition alone? This had all happened when Dave was at home—not me—and yet I was the one left defending our collective innocence. That weekend, after Schuyler's fall in the basement and subsequent behavior (which we fortunately got on tape), Dave seemed to have a better understanding of what I had been telling him about for years. That realization was nice but cold comfort as I waited to see what would unfold next.

Just hours after the social worker's phone call, I heard a knock on the door. I saw a woman at my front door, holding her Illinois State government badge, and the situation became real.

"DCFS," she said, knocking loudly and trying to peek in through the window to the left of the door. "Mrs. Walker, I'm Janice Whitney with DCFS. May I come in?"

Could she come in? Did I have a choice? I opened the front door, holding a three-year-old Sloane on my hip. "Please, call me Christine," I said. "Come in."

Janice asked me question after question about Dave,

me, our marriage, and the kids. The questions began to feel more like an interrogation than an interview. Her tone reeked of her suspicion that I might be covering for an abusive husband.

"Come here, son." Janice motioned Connor over to the table. He ran over, still in his pajamas. "Connor, right?" She smiled for the first time.

Connor nodded.

"You know what happened to your brother, Schuyler, right?" she asked.

Connor nodded.

Janice reached into her handbag and pulled out a piece of paper with the front and back of a body outline—something right out of a coroner's report. She laid it on the dining room table, where we had been sitting for the past ten minutes.

"Draw an X where your daddy hit your brother," she prompted, handing Connor a pencil.

Where your daddy hit your brother? She had to be kidding me! So now, our family would be added the list of child beaters and crack heads that throw their infants out of tenth floor windows and leave their seven kids under the age of five alone, in diapers, hungry, filthy, and crawling around a dirt floor covered in roaches while they go out drinking? I understood that there were people who were unequipped to become parents, who had children who needed protection from harm and neglect. DAVE AND I WERE NOT AMONG THEM. I could feel the blood drain from my head through to my feet at the prospect of needing to prove my innocence to someone who had never met me.

Connor looked uncomprehendingly at Janice, holding

the crayon limply in his hand until he shrugged, turned his attention to something else, and skipped out of the room. I looked at Janice, waiting for her to apologize, but she merely arranged her papers and asked (and by asked, I mean insisted) on a tour of the house. I felt like a student eager to get a good grade. Since we were sitting right off the kitchen, I opened the refrigerator door to show her the array of organic foods, fresh produce, and healthy snacks. I showed her the locks we had on cabinets to keep cleaning chemicals out of reach. I pointed out the photos on the fridge of family outings to pumpkin farms and train depots. I showed her the back yard, which was completely fenced in and had a swing set, and pointed to the police and fire station across the street. As we were walking upstairs to the second floor, I offered that we didn't smoke, rarely drank (so there was no alcohol cabinet to worry about), and did not have guns in the house. I was happy to show her the house, especially the children's rooms, which I had painstakingly decorated and arranged to create little havens for each of them.

"Why are there locks on the doors?" she asked.

"Sometimes when Schuyler is out of control, I have the kids go to their rooms and I lock their doors from the outside so he can't get in. I want to keep them safe," I responded, but as she began writing notes from the pad she pulled from her handbag, I knew it was the wrong answer.

"You can't lock your kids in their rooms," she said.

"Then what can I do?" I asked her. *Tell me what I can do when my second grader is wreaking havoc in the house and I want to protect my younger children!* I'd hidden my knives. I'd put away everything I could think of that might be a weapon, but I still never knew what Schuyler might attempt. And, as diligent as I wanted to be, I simply couldn't watch everyone every minute of the day. Connor and Schuyler might each be in their rooms, playing with toys, and suddenly I'd hear Connor scream because Schuyler had barged in and started throwing stuff at him. Or Sloane might be down for a nap and Schuyler would open the door and wake her intentionally, sending her into inconsolable wails.

"What should I do?" I asked her again, genuinely hoping for an answer.

"Well, you can't do *that!*" was all she said, pointing to the locks.

I watched Janice closely, but I couldn't see an inch of softness, one glint of understanding. She was trained to look for instances of child abuse and neglect. And because that's what she looked for, that was what she would see. She wasn't used to looking for mental illness, especially in a child, so she would never believe me. But she had the power to make a monumental decision about my family. She could decide the bruise on Schuyler's face indicated abuse. She could say the locks on the door indicated a larger pattern of abuse or neglect. She could take one or even all of my children away from me. My legs shook as this thought sunk in. I could lose my children. As she wrapped up the visit, she reminded me she wanted to talk with Dave when he returned. Even after that, it would still take several weeks before we would receive her findings.

Once she left, I sank down into the dining room chair, staring at the papers she had left behind. The shaking that began in my legs traveled through the rest of my body; I swear I shook for days. I couldn't eat. The idea of food made me nauseous, and my hand shook so much that it was impossible to even get a fork in my mouth. The only thing that stopped the shaking was a sip of white wine. At eleven in the morning. Thank God, we didn't have any place we needed to be and I could still function.

I knew one thing for sure: we couldn't go on like this. Our family could not survive this constant threat. We were failing and needed a solution fast. The very fiber of our family unit was at risk, and I was not about to see my children placed in foster homes.

As parents, particularly as moms, we like to think we can provide our children everything they need to succeed. I had tried that with Schuyler. But the special diets, the specific vitamins, the counseling, the medicines— they simply were not enough to help his brain. From his success at school, it was clear that he did better in a structured environment, but he needed it throughout the day, every day, and not just at school. Schuyler needed it at home. Despite my efforts, with two other children, there was no way to provide the kind of structure he needed. This was bigger than I was. No matter what we did or tried to do, we failed, and I knew it would not get easier the older Schuyler got.

"He can't live here," I said out loud. I was not losing my family over this illness. I could not, and would not, let this illness break up our family. We had only one other option: a therapeutic boarding school.

*"Beware how you take away hope
from another human being."*
—Justice Oliver Wendell Holmes

"Aim high in hope and work."
—Daniel Burnham

CHAPTER 6
WHY I STILL CHASE HOPE

You get a lot of funny looks when people find out your seven-year-old son is in a residential therapeutic school. "How could you send him away when he's so young?" they wonder. Aside from not "sending him away," I knew that Schuyler was going to benefit through intensive supports we simply could not provide in our home. While it is not typical and we missed him, how could we not pursue the best course of treatment?

After that day in June 2007, when DCFS came to our house, I realized several truths about our lives. Schuyler needed more structure and expertise. I also needed to make sure everyone stayed safe. The woman from DCFS didn't understand and didn't try. Instead, she admonished me and reminded me—and Dave, too, when she met him later, that if Schuyler harmed either of the kids, Dave and I would bear the responsibility for his actions. If Schuyler harmed himself or got hurt, we would also bear the responsibility. Even as Dave and I each asked the social worker for answers or suggestions, for some kind of lifeline, she just made thinly veiled threats. It was obvious that she was not familiar with the signs of mental illness, so she only looked for the signs she could recognize from child abuse and neglect. I knew in my heart that if Schuyler or one of the other children got hurt, not only would some horrid outcome be part of the story, but I could also lose all of my children to foster care. I had an obligation to Sloane and Connor to give them a childhood without the chaos that often ruled our home.

Schuyler was at Camp Buckskin for the month of July, during which he celebrated his seventh birthday. While he was gone, our family had our first taste of normalcy: days spent going to the beach at the spur of the moment, playing in the park without worrying about what run-ins we might have with playmates, and going a whole day without hearing someone cry or anything breaking. Once, Connor turned to Dave and said, "Hey, Dad, I didn't get hit by Schuyler today." As sad as that was, it rang true. We got to experience the other side. So this was how other parents felt! *This is a piece of cake!* I thought. *I enjoy this.*

A few weeks later, we received the final response from DCFS, and they concluded there was "no finding" of child abuse, which meant that our case was dismissed after being investigated. But now, a foundation had been laid, and any other incidents would only escalate DCFS' involvement. For years, I had visions that something awful would happen at home, which would be on the news with the story ending, ". . . and DCFS had prior contact with the family." My heart could not handle it, and my head would not allow that to be our family's fate.

I had first considered a residential school when Schuyler was five years old, but I didn't pursue it. Like most families, we instead tried just about everything under the sun, hoping that the next thing would sweep all our troubles away. I told myself that as Schuyler got older, life would even out a bit. How could it not? He was five, for God's sake! But every episode, every tantrum, every three-day weekend of counting the minutes until the next school day made me understand that this was real, and it wasn't getting better as Schuyler got older. It was getting worse.

Professionals say that most parents have a two-year lag between first thinking about a residential school and enrolling their child in one. That was us, almost to the day. As I was getting ready to move Schuyler into a residential program, I talked with many parents who already had children living in therapeutic schools. I asked for their advice, direction, and overall tips for moving ahead.

As I spoke with each of these families, one common sentiment was echoed: why did we wait? *Why did we wait to get Sean into the best treatment possible? Why did we think Matthew would get better on his own? How much further could our Susan have gotten both emotionally and socially if we had sought a residential placement when she was thirteen instead of seventeen?*

Why is it that a child has to endure hospitalizations, school suspensions, and suicide attempts in order to "prove" their needs are as real as those who have conditions that can be definitively detected through traditional diagnostics? Parents told me, without exception, that they wished they had made the move to residential treatment when their son or daughter was Schuyler's age.

Hearing that confirmed my gut feeling that this was a move we had to make, both for Schuyler and for every member of our family. This was no longer about getting through a tough night or managing spring break moment by moment, leaving behind a trail of exhaustion, pain, and despair. This was about finding a better way, a better outcome for Schuyler and for our family. On this, Dave and I agreed.

By the time Schuyler returned from camp, I had already visited the Orthogenic School in the Hyde Park area of Chicago. I had met with the admissions staff and arranged to return with Schuyler for the final phase of the application process. Having researched what was available, what was appropriate, and what would be paid for, I decided that the O School, as it is known, was our best option.

In searching for the right residential program placement, parents need to look at many different factors: what is the student population the school serves? Some programs are co-ed, some are single gender; some schools accept children as young as five (as the O School does), while other schools are for high school-aged children only. What is the philosophy of the school and treatment program?

It is so crucial to find the right fit, as not all therapeutic boarding schools are created equal. Let me repeat that: *not all therapeutic boarding schools are created equal*. This is unlike, say, an auto repair shop or tax preparer where almost anywhere you go, you can find someone who knows what to do, has the tools to complete the job, and will give you a comparable outcome, give or take. With a therapeutic boarding school, the atmosphere, the culture, and the attitude of the staff—beyond the school's statistics or philosophy—can make the difference between success and failure.

What can make the selection of the right program so tough is that there are so few of them! Because this pool is so small, many families must fly across the country to enroll their son or daughter in the right program. More often than not, the distance involved can cloud a family's decision to go the residential route, even though it might offer their child the best chance for future success. It is totally understandable. While an eighteen-year-old heading off to college ten states away is typical, it can seem counterintuitive when it comes to an eleven-year-old girl or seven-year-old boy. In the eyes of some, such a move can be seen as "sending them away," but if a child is sent to an established boarding school on the East Coast, few people bat an eyelash. It is helpful for families who are hesitant or who would prefer to eliminate any possible trauma of separation (both for them and their child) to see this decision as one that is medically necessary. If your son or daughter had some horrid disease, you would most likely spend hours online finding the world's noted authority on that disease, call and beg for an appointment, and buy plane tickets.

Mental illness can't be seen on a diagnostic test the way a brain tumor or abnormal white blood count can. This can make it easier to delay the decision, telling ourselves that maybe this behavior will even out on its own or that our son or daughter will grow out of this phase. You will try just one more diet, one more therapy, one more doctor, one more service animal, one more medication, one more whatever. This reasoning, or bargaining with God, is also normal. I mean, who wants to be among a group of affected parents who often feel they must meet in secret? Let me say this as gently as I can:

living in denial is no way to live. Like covering your eyes and insisting no one can see you, the truth is there and patiently waiting for you to act.

Making the decision to pursue the right fit of residential placement is the hardest part. It is the high point of the roller coaster just before you begin the ninety-degree drop. Each person has a different timetable coming to that realization. When parents say they aren't sure if residential is really needed, what that probably means is that life hasn't gotten bad enough. Maybe one parent gets to that place before the other parent does (which can be incredibly trying on a marriage and even worse after a contentious divorce). Sometimes the epiphany comes after an awful (even harmful) event, when the family reflects and says, "We just can't live like this anymore." Regardless of the timing, when it comes to making the move, a parent usually feels a sense of relief, as in "Ah, there is a reason to smile again, and life is about to change for the better." That sentiment alone made me feel better. Doing what you have always done, while expecting a different result, is foolish; Dave and I were confident in the knowledge that we had tried everything available to us, and yet we could not meet Schuyler's needs at home. While I would miss Schuyler, I would not miss the chaos.

One thing that was essential in our selection of the O School was that it was truly therapeutic in nature. We did not want any kind of warehousing or custodial care, or for Schuyler to live with children who wound up in residential care as a means of diversion from the juvenile justice system. Also, we wanted to make sure the school provided an outstanding education in addition to supportive living arrangements. Not all residential centers contain a school, and not all therapeutic schools have residential components, so having both in one was a key consideration.

While investigating a few options, it became clear that the expectations for students and their families were measurably higher at the O School than at other facilities. In addition, the standards for hiring staff were incredible stringent; a master's degree is required to apply for a staff position. Also, we found that every member of the school and residential sides of the O School wanted to work there—not one person "wound up" there because he or she was unsure about career choices. Every year, the O School has more applicants than open positions, and staff and leadership alike pride themselves on the effectiveness of the relational approach to treatment over other treatments (such as behavioral, or motivating by fear or force). The culture of the O School is one of excellence, accountability, transparency, facilitated growth, positive outcomes, and community partnerships. The staff is in the business of transforming lives, and they are all in! Just as different corporations have different cultures, norms, and expectations, so do residential therapeutic schools. As such, you must find a culture that fits you and your family, as well as what treatment approach speaks to you most.

Another aspect of treatment that you should consider is the role of the family. Some schools engage families at a high level by incorporating a parents' association (like a PTO) and regularly planned family events (such as a brunch, a dorm open house, or a prom); regular and detailed communication about activities or internal changes; mandated family therapy; and encouraged family visits, phone calls (or Skype and FaceTime for families who are far from school), and mail. Other therapeutic schools are less focused on making sure that clients and their families are working through issues that arise due to the complicated nature of autism or mental illness. Some organizations have been created to fill the void of displaced children who have had painful beginnings in life and lack a strong and supportive family foundation. As such, if there is no family to engage, or if expectations for children are low and prospects for future success are perceived as bleak, the programming, staffing, and growth opportunities might reflect that. Finally, when students turn eighteen or twenty-one, it is key to understand what transition planning has been established to support them in their next steps into adulthood. Is college in the picture? Where will they live? Are they able to hold a full-time job?

In short, please make sure that you have a very good understanding of any school's policies before you enroll your child, including:

- The school's philosophy toward treatment.
- Expectations of family involvement.
- Standards in hiring staff.
- Discharge planning.
- Established communications.
- Visitation policies.
- Crisis intervention strategies.
- Parental involvement in medical, dental, and psychiatric decisions.
- Dispute resolution.

- Structure of receiving and sending mail and phone calls.
- Frequency and quality of family therapy provided.
- Nutritional offering.
- Recreational opportunities.
- The existence of a family support network or parent association where families can connect.

Each of these elements will play a role in daily life for your family, and it is it crucial that you are comfortable with the answers to these questions. If you are not, keep looking!

Once a good fit is identified, then the process of getting in begins, which can be predicated on whether a family has funding or not. So, more conversations: who will pay? Does the school district agree with the need for a residential program? Does insurance cover the placement at school? Is any public funding available, and how do you get it? These are the questions that families looking to find the right placement and program for their child must face, dealing with different levels of government and educators, all while continuing to meet the demands on their time every day. Think of the college selection process times a gajillion; add more invasive questions than a mortgage application; and then factor in waiting, rejection, and plan B . . . and you begin to have a sense as to what the initial process is like. It's enough to make me need a nap! And that's all before the child moves in!

But I knew it was worth it. Just looking at how Schuyler had thrived at camp removed any doubt I may have had. It was beautiful to see him looking so healthy, relaxed, and happy. That first day back, he was incredibly regulated—it was the best day we had with all three kids in all of 2007. I took a photo of Schuyler, Connor, and Sloane that day at the Chicago Botanic Garden, huddled amongst each other with tons of glorious flowers behind them. They were looking into the camera and smiling. For that instant, I felt in balance. I keep that framed photo in Schuyler's bedroom.

Over the years, I have joked that our life is Camelot, but not because of any JFK similarities. Rather, because for one, brief, shining moment, the Walkers were normal. It is these moments that I treasure and remind myself of when the light turns to darkness.

The night after Schuyler came back from camp, Dave and I told him that we had some good news for him. We had just finished eating dinner and walked out to the screened-in porch in front of our house. Dave and I sat on each side of Schuyler to share the news.

"Sky, you know how you loved sleepover camp?" I began.

Schuyler nodded, smiling. His cheeks had a beautiful summer tan.

"Well, we found a sleepover school, and you get to go!" I made it sound like a positive—which it was.

"Okay," Schuyler said.

"It will be like camp, but it's closer to home so we can see each other during the school year. Here are some pictures." Dave showed Schuyler photos of the school—the front of the building, the dorm he would live in—that I had taken the day I visited so that Schuyler would have a visual to match his thoughts.

A slow smile spread across Schuyler's face. "Can I put up posters?" he asked.

"Absolutely! We'll have fun making your room the way you want it," I assured him.

Schuyler was excited about it, no doubt recalling his great summer camp experience. Dave and I exchanged relieved smiles of our own over Schuyler's head as he bent to examine the photos more closely. He had responded so well. We didn't talk about any of the incidents at home or school or in any way convey that this was a parting of the ways or punishment. We stressed that this was something Schuyler *got* to do, not *had* to do.

We were extremely fortunate. Few therapeutic residential programs exist for kids like Schuyler, and many parents have to take a plane to the nearest one. But the O School was just a forty-five-minute drive from our house, and we could visit him whenever we wished. We are a family of five, not of four. We have three children, not one. It was important for us to feel that even though Schuyler would receive his mail at a different address, he would still know in his heart that he is part of our family.

The day after our talk, we drove down to school for our final interview. Thankfully, it was a formality, and a date was set for moving in—September 28, a Friday. It was the miracle we needed.

• • •

Before Schuyler went to the O School, Connor and Sloane had grown accustomed to the trauma and chaos that accompanied most days. Now, with Schuyler not living at home, we could focus on brief visits that kept us connected but were finite and usually fun. It was important to me that Connor and Sloane saw their brother in a positive light—that they continued to love him and better understand his limitations. There were certainly some hurt feelings that would heal, but the main goal was to have healthy, happy, balanced, and secure children who could emerge stronger for having experienced challenges so early on.

When Connor and Sloane thought of their brother, I wanted them to remember the fun they had on our many visits and to be able to separate the brother they love from the behavior they do not. There were so many activities! The O School, being incredibly committed to a deep sense of family engagement, hosts events for families every six weeks or so throughout the year. From bingo and spaghetti lunches to the Father's Day barbecue to a formal prom in May, our family was constantly attending events together at the O School in addition to our regular trips to visit Schuyler.

We felt as though we were part of a larger family in every sense of the word. The Parents' Association held regular meetings as a means of support, information sharing, and event planning. Having the name, email address, and phone number of every family enrolled at the school was a terrific way to reach out to others who were in the exact same boat. There was no need to explain a thing; just share empathy and solutions, which few other outsiders seemed to have. While friends and colleagues could listen, they could not truly grasp the extent of our challenges, nor could they provide answers to our many questions. Knowing that another family is going through what you are is like being wrapped in a blanket fresh out of the dryer. Ahh . . . I'm not alone.

At the O School, with structure, therapy, medicine, and the support of the school staff and our family, Schuyler made incredible progress. After four years, he was ready for the next step in residential treatment, including a higher level of behavioral expectations, greater independent living opportunities, and increased community involvement. However, the O School couldn't offer that for Schuyler because of his young age. The next classroom and dorm openings were two years away, and at that point, Schuyler had been in the same boys' dorm and elementary school classroom since the age of seven. He had seen countless kids come in and move out while he was still there. There was some worry that Schuyler might become less engaged if he began thinking he would not leave the program himself or that he would never "graduate" to another level. So, in summer of 2011, the work to find another residential program for him began.

After a few weeks of searching, we found Genesee Lake School in Wisconsin, then known as Oconomowoc Developmental Treatment Center (ODTC). Genesee Lake School (GLS) is a year-round special education school that provides developmentally appropriate educational and vocational services to students, both in a day school and in a residential setting. As is the case with its peers, GLS focuses heavily on providing Common Core State Standards that are driven by an Individualized Education Plan (IEP) and required by the IDEA (the Individuals with Disabilities Education Act), which is a federal standard for educating students with differences. Set in a gorgeous wooded area surrounded by lakes (an outdoorsman's dream!), GLS is about twenty-five miles west of Milwaukee. Although this was farther from our house at a travel time of two hours, it was still the closest and best option for us. The fact that many of the other residential students traveled much farther was not lost on us. Another huge plus: GLS was an approved facility by the

State of Illinois, which meant we could transfer Schuyler's funding to GLS without a protracted battle with the State of Illinois.

Dave and I agreed that Schuyler was ready for the next step in his treatment and thought that GLS's educational curriculum and structure could offer what he needed. Fortunately, GLS had space for Schuyler in their program. He would also have his own room, which was a huge plus after sharing a large room with up to six other boys. We took it as a good sign that the number on his room was #23, as in the date of his birthday in July and the now-retired jersey number of Bulls legend Michael Jordan, someone near and dear to Chicago sports fans. Since GLS came highly recommended, we didn't think twice about moving Schuyler in.

What impressed us right away was the caliber of the educational team. GLS's special education teachers were incredibly attuned to Schuyler's strengths and needs. The school was in a shiny new building that had an entrance with inspirational quotes painted on the walls. Schuyler was in good educational hands and, with this support, making the academic progress his IEP outlined. Schuyler's teachers sent weekly emails about how the prior week went, and I in turn let them know how our weekend visits had gone so the team had a good sense of our successes or any issues that had arisen during our time together. GLS also had nice rooms perfect for family day visits, complete with a TV/DVD player. The staff could also arrange for meals from the cafeteria to be brought back to the room during a family visit.

The following summer, Schuyler turned twelve and was then eligible to move to a less-structured group home setting. We jumped at the chance to have Schuyler move out of a dormitory and dining hall environment and experience living in a home setting. Cheryl House, as it is called, was for boys up to age eighteen, who were supported by a 24/7 GLS staff. Daily schedules, community outings, and relationship building with housemates were stressed, along with independent living skills. Each boy was responsible for doing his own laundry, cleaning parts of the house, and helping with grocery shopping and meal preparation. They even had a baking night each Monday, when the staff introduced a new recipe and helped the boys learn how to create easy and delicious meals.

Still, we missed being able to see Schuyler more frequently and hoped for an opportunity to bring him closer to home again. In the summer of 2013, the Orthogenic School created a new middle school classroom, and previously unavailable space opened up in its middle school dorm for boys. Schuyler was invited to return. We were thrilled to have him so close to us (in the same state at least!) and in a place that suited his needs so well. On October 8, 2013, Schuyler became only the second child in recent memory to return to the O School after being discharged. In the fall of 2014, he will start high school and most likely return to our community. This means attending a therapeutic day school and residing in a supportive home with other boys who also attend the local therapeutic school. Schuyler's attendance in any residential placement is only possible because of a grant we get from the Illinois Department of Human Services, Division of Mental Health, to help cover tuition. If the grant is ever denied through the annual renewal process, I'm not sure what we'll do.

For all of our progress, we still live with uncertainty. We don't know what Schuyler's future looks like. He's a teenager now, and hormones can affect him even more, throwing off the delicate balance we've established. Will that balance hold? What will he be like at eighteen? Will he be able to go to college? Will he be able to live independently? He loves to design and build things. Can he find a career he loves and in which he finds meaning? What will that mean for him and for our family?

Speaking of our family, what effects will our challenges have on our other children? Sure, I've seen a deep level of compassion from Sloane and Connor that truly makes me proud, but both of them have told me that they deeply resent the chaos Schuyler causes and the time and energy Dave and I must commit to his treatment. And what about Dave and me? God knows we've had our horrible times, and we've made it through, but we just don't know what lies ahead. Although we all live with uncertainty, when you have a child with mental illness or autism, the ramifications of uncertainty are much greater. It sucks not to know what the future holds, but I can either let that suffocate me or I can chase hope. I choose to chase hope.

• • •

Chasing hope, to me, means seeing the glass as half full and always believing there is another chance to fill it when it tips over. Chasing hope is running toward a crisis, emboldened by the confidence forged by challenge and the mastery that has been gifted by experience. Chasing hope means staying abreast of the latest and greatest innovations in medicine and policy but not holding our breath thinking that one discovery will make every hardship vanish. Chasing hope doesn't mean ignoring the horridness of everything we've been through; it means creating something beautiful out of it. When people go through a crisis, it's normal to grieve for the old way of life. When you have a beautiful four-year-old who just happens to be diagnosed with autism, ADHD, and mood disorder, it's understandable to yearn for that alternate reality of a healthy, perfect baby, and life—the one you imagined when you were pregnant.

Just as the homeowner stands outside the ashes of her ravaged home, fervently wishing for everything to be return to normal, parents of children with mental illness or autism can get stuck in the anger, frustration, and fear that come from realizing they have yet another day of being them. Some parents get stuck in denial, where they chase a hope that's fruitless, trying any and every so-called miracle cure that, in the end, only leaves the family more distraught and drained of resources. Chasing hope, though, means recognizing that a fire has swept through your house, that a diagnosis has altered your life, that your child is never going to live a "normal" life, but that you will still be okay. It's accepting what has happened and figuring out the best possible outcome. It's not just *going* through it but *growing* through it. It's accepting your own "life fire" and then picking up the pieces to rebuild and embrace the future.

The hope I chase is that we continue to help Schuyler's brain grow and develop so he can live a productive, healthy, meaningful, and happy life. I hope he is able to channel his passion and gifts into a profession that honors his talents and gives him profound fulfillment. That ideal life is the same thing I wish for Sloane and Connor.

I hope doctors can someday diagnose mental illness through a definitive test, like an MRI or blood or urine screening, and they can say with conviction exactly what condition the person is battling. I hope these doctors and the rest of the medical community develop the compassion to understand what families like ours deal with every minute, not just when we are in their offices. I hope more doctors specialize in pediatric mental health so people all over the country, all over the world, have access to this care and not just those who are fortunate enough to live in larger cities.

I hope legislators comprehend how certain laws cause families to make impossible choices, such as relinquishing custody of their children in order to receive funding for treatment in a residential community.

I really want the health care and insurance system to understand how essential it is to provide therapy and medicine to children with mental illness early in their lives, when the most improvement can be made. The "wait and see" approach does by far more harm than good. I want the medication and therapies people living with mental illness need to be affordable, so no family has to make a choice between treatment and life essentials.

I'd like the educational system to recognize the requirements of children with mental illness and autism and have different programs to meet different needs. I hope teachers have patience with the child who constantly misbehaves despite his best efforts not to and have compassion for the families that deal with that behavior all of the time, not just during the school day. I hope stakeholders can stop litigating their way to a child's academic and social success. Let's call a spade a spade and make the goal more about succeeding by a child's own definition than by societal norms.

And for fellow parents? I hope you find others who understand and accept what you are going through and offer support in the traditional ways people comfort others. I want you to talk openly about the struggles and triumphs you face. I want you to have ready access to the information and resources you need to make the best decisions about your child's care. Please know that this kind of illness strikes every walk of life, and you did nothing to bring your child's illness on. Nothing. But it does take more than love. Trust your instincts and fight like hell.

I hope this book is a start. By reading my story, may you see that you're not alone. It's hard. Really hard. But there are also moments of unexpected joy, and those must be celebrated.

Our paths may be different, but our journey to find help and hope for our children is the same. In the thirteen years since Schuyler was born, I've learned a hell of a lot. The most important lessons are the ones that I'm passing on to you, hoping they might ease your own bumpy road.

"I don't think of the misery,
but the beauty that still remains."
—Anne Frank

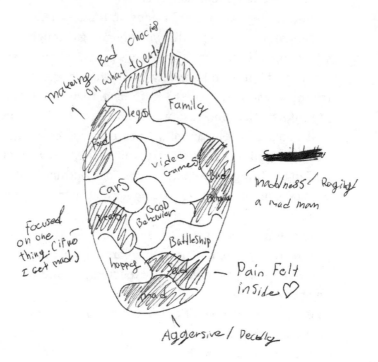

5-13% my Brain

making Bad choices on what to eat

legos
Family
Food
video games
Bad Behavior
cars
Good Behavior
peace
madness/ Raging/ a mad man
Battleship
happy
sad
mad
Pain Felt inside ♡
focused on one thing (if no I Get mad)
Aggersive/ Deadly

Art: Schuyler m.

See, this is my Brain, yelling consecures. Do not help.

One of Schuyler's greatest strengths is his ability to create original drawings. Schuyler created these four drawings when he was asked what it's like to have his brain. As you can see, Schuyler outlined how different parts of his brain focus on different things and how he describes his "good brain" and his "bad brain."

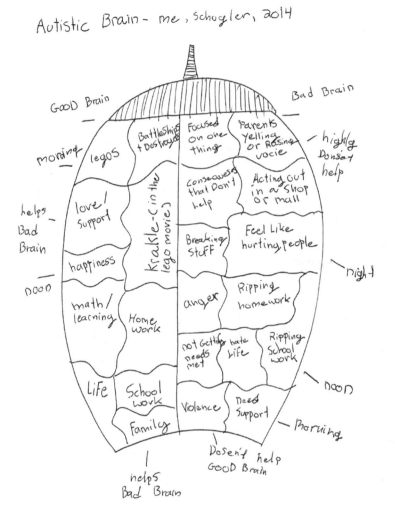

Also, Schuyler depicts things that help him feel better or make him feel worse, and offers solutions on how those around him can best meet his needs. Seeing how Schuyler views the world and what causes certain desires and emotions is essential to understanding how to best support him.

Sad / mad Behavors

mad Because I DiDent
Get what I want

Fist's = Puching

that's a

nono

if this your
child lethim
play video Games
or calm himDown

happy Side

not mad

Thatsa
meme

no Fisests
Relaxed Arms

this is higly
Relaxing For
Chilbern.

And baby makes three! Bringing Schuyler home from the hospital, July 2000.

Dave and Schuyler enjoying play time at home, 2001. This is one of our favorite photos.

Kids giving Dave their Father's Day present to him, 2006.

Schuyler's first
day of first grade
at North Shore
Academy, 2006.

Formal
proms at
the O School,
2008 and
2009.

Visiting with former Congressman John Porter on one of our lobbying trips to Washington, D.C., 2010. John has been a champion for neuroscience research for decades. The John Edward Porter Neuroscience Research Center at the National Institutes of Health (NIH) opened in 2013. John is my public policy mentor, role model, and inspiration.

Enjoying a day visit at the O School, 2010.

O School graduation day, August 2011.

Schuyler at the Chicago Sky game, 2011.

The team's mascot is Sky Guy, a nickname Schuyler has had since birth.

Schuyler hugging with Scout on one of our overnight visits in Wisconsin, 2012.

"Hope is not about outcomes."
—Anonymous

TEN THINGS I WISH I'D KNOWN BEFORE I BECAME THE PARENT OF A CHILD WITH A BRAIN DISORDER

As a tribute to Maria Shriver, I have created my own Top Ten list of things I wish I had known when Schuyler's challenges first surfaced. Just as Shriver reflected on her own college graduation day as she prepared remarks for a commencement speech, citing the ten things she wished she had known before heading out as an adult in the real world, I have a list of things I wish I had been told before my average life met a fork in the road to my new normal. In that same spirit, I'm sharing with you what I needed to know prior to 2002 and what you may need to know now. These lessons came through real experiences—some horrid, some hysterical—and I hope they help you feel better prepared and able to captain your own ship.

1. A Funny Thing Happens on the Way to Happily Ever After
2. Siblings are People, Too (or Why Every Woman Should Be Elastigirl)
3. Why My M.O.M. Trumps Your M.D.
4. Don't Throw Good Money after Bad
5. The Only Thing Constant is Change
6. With Every Breakdown Comes a Breakthrough
7. It's Only Weird If It Doesn't Work
8. Beware the Mama Grizzly
9. Anne Sullivan Was a Saint
10. Holland Isn't Such a Bad Place

1: A FUNNY THING HAPPENS ON THE WAY TO HAPPILY EVER AFTER

It's written in the wedding vows and for a very good reason: "For better or worse." Remember that one? Yeah, I said it, too. After all, what could be that bad? I envisioned saying "I do" and going off to face the world with Dave, taking down hurdles and growing stronger with each victory! Isn't that the bill of goods young girls are sold? From Bridal Barbie to the four-pound wedding magazines, so much emphasis is placed on the wedding day rather than the actual marriage. Forget the china and his and hers towels—there should be a registry for couple's and family therapy!

The most important decision a person can make is choosing a spouse. This far exceeds career choice, city of residence, and educational path, as your spouse (hopefully) is by your side regardless of what you are doing with your time and where you are doing it. Seasoned couples often advise young lovers to choose wisely. If the divorce rate in the general population hovers around 50 percent, it is in the 80–90 percent range (depending on the source) for couples that have a child with special needs. If daily life can knock you down, add to that caring for a child who needs additional support in order to do the most basic of things. That can add up to a soul-crushing siege that threatens your ability to keep your marriage intact.

A few years back, as I began to write this book, I surveyed countless couples that had children with special needs and asked them how raising their child affected their marriage. The results were consistent and eye opening.

Some of the women who completed the survey said that the stress created by raising their affected child was a contributing factor in their divorce. Some women admitted that their husbands "just couldn't handle it" and left. Other women confided that they lived in sexless marriages, as the extra attention, effort, and patience required to raise their child, or children, took every ounce of energy they had. Still others told me that sex was the last thing on their minds after a day of fighting school districts, shuttling kids to doctor's appointments, or cleaning up the three dozen raw eggs that their autistic son had thrown around the kitchen that morning. For all of these women, getting through an average day took mental gymnastics just to stay at baseline.

Coming in a close second to stress as a contributing factor in divorce is the blame game. Whose fault is it? "Well, your family's genes caused this, you know!" Or, "If you hadn't done such and such, this wouldn't have happened!" Sound familiar? Sure does . . . but why? Aren't couples supposed to circle the wagons and not shoot toward the center? While some couples are able to rise to the occasion, others disintegrate under the relentless pressure of daily life. At times, raising a child with profound needs can suck all of the joy out of parenting. When chaos or strife hits a fever pitch, it is common for tempers to flare, expletives to fly, and blame to be thrown.

In the end, though, it is all about parenting what has come your way, regardless of the route it took.

Families who have adopted babies that they already knew had challenges don't seem to play the blame game, as they voluntarily took on the additional responsibility.

Most of the couples I talked to who became parents through adoption told me that they felt honored to be the difference in their child's life, adding that in the case of foreign adoption, their sons or daughters would have had a much lower quality of life had they remained in their native country. All of the couples I spoke with had the financial means to support their children for decades to come, and some had already been parents to biological children. Only a few couples confided that the caring of their adopted children was much more difficult than they had originally anticipated. Those couples did not expect the specialty schools, respite care, and clinical interventions that raising their children would require. And the families that adopted children without having a medical history of the birth parents, only to learn later of their child's special needs, felt blindsided.

I found the issue of medication to be another common source of contention among the couples I surveyed. Dave and I certainly disagreed initially on the recommended course of treatment for Schuyler. Some women reported that their husbands (or ex-husbands) refused to acknowledge that their child even had a challenge. Over the years, I have come to believe that fathers often have a harder time accepting that their child, especially a biological son, is anything short of perfect. It can be too much for a father to admit that maybe a child he helped create won't be the quarterback at Notre Dame or CEO of IBM. Dads are used to fixing things, and these kinds of challenges can't be fixed. Instead, they must be acknowledged, accepted, and (ideally) embraced. This doesn't make dads bad guys; it just means it can take them longer to get to same point as moms.

These parenting challenges can deeply affect a marriage. When two people are exhausted, stressed, scared, and angry over their child's situation, it's too easy to vent on the person standing in the trenches with you. Alternatively, it's also too easy to assume that your partner, the love of your life, should just automatically understand what you're going through, and if he doesn't, it's an indication that he doesn't care.

The Real Deal Takeaway: Don't believe the fairytale wedding hype. Having a child with mental illness or autism will challenge your marriage in ways you cannot imagine, and you'll need to change your approach to problem solving in order to cope and to ensure your relationship survives. You may need to learn to communicate with your spouse differently than before. You may have to check in with each other and be very clear on what your needs and expectations are—even if you think they should be obvious. You will constantly have to put your child's needs above your own, but you'll also have to know when you need to draw the line and take a moment to recharge—and when and how to ask for help. Some couples consider marriage counseling a must during this time, not because the marriage is weak but because it is about to go into crisis, and getting the tools to bolster it can only help. Your roles may change, with one of you becoming the primary caretaker. At times, it won't feel fair. It won't be fair. But it may be what's needed. If you are the primary caregiver, make a concerted effort to involve your partner. Schedule doctors' appointments and school conferences when you can both go. Assume you'll both be involved, and seek to make decisions together.

If you're not the primary caregiver, don't assume everything is just fine because your partner seems to be handling everything. Your partner may be madly juggling many balls, making it look easy, even though it's not. Assume you'll go with your spouse to the appointments and meetings with clinicians. If you cannot, ask about them afterwards, remembering that you're seeking information instead of Monday morning quarterbacking. Remember that it's going to be challenging at times—so when you find that it is, don't think it's just *your* marriage. It's the situation, so expect that, and have a realistic view of your relationship. That way, you'll be better able to anticipate the bumpy roads and know that those bumps are *normal*. The most important thing is to support each other—you may not have too many other people who will do that, so you have to pay special attention to doing it for each other. Most of all, remember to embrace what you do have versus what you don't.

> *"Hope is the dream of a waking man."*
> —Aristotle

2: SIBLINGS ARE PEOPLE, TOO (OR WHY EVERY WOMAN SHOULD BE ELASTIGIRL)

I was an only child raised by a single mom for most of my youth, so sibling rivalry is completely lost on me. Totally. I mean, I just don't get it. The fights over who finishes dinner first or who gets to the car first are beyond me. I hate seeing the tears of the "loser" and the end-zone dance of the "winner." Since when did eating one's mac and cheese become a contest? And aren't we all going to the same place in the same car, so why does it matter who touches the car first? And the "calling" of the front seat? What is that? Or how the first thing one sibling does when they are given something is to ask or look at what the other sibling has been given? I can buy the same book at the same store in the same transaction and each sibling will still want what the other has! Give me strength.

So it is only natural that when a sibling with special needs is in the mix, the fight for attention from parents can become a cage match. And when a sibling's challenges are behavioral in nature, there can be countless episodes of, shall we say, unpleasantness they must endure.

In the movie *The Incredibles*, mom Helen Parr (aka Elastigirl) is able to stretch herself into almost any shape and length in order to get just about any job done. Whether she is trying to land her stowaway brood safely into the ocean, break up a fight at the dinner table, or be in two rooms at once, she can do it. I believe that all women should have Elastigirl capabilities. It would sure make it easier to meet very different demands, which usually present themselves at the exact same moment.

When it comes to managing sibling relationships, both as the kids relate to each other and as they interact with me, I often find myself at a loss. There are three of them and one of me. Someone's hand can't be held crossing the street. I can't be at one child's football game, be at another's scout meeting, and visit the third two hours away all in the same afternoon. Believe me: I've tried, but the laws of time and space win out every time.

If the 80/20 rule in business applies to families, 80 percent of a parent's time will be spent with the child who has greater needs than with the child whose needs can be met without additional effort. It's just the way it works. In families without any challenges, if one person gets the flu or breaks a leg, the attention of the house focuses on that person until he or she is well, with others picking up the slack and adjusting schedules. Now imagine a flu that never subsides or a broken bone that never heals. The attention ratio is forever disproportionate, and siblings can feel the brunt of it for years.

Using another business analogy, it's like the district manager who never visits the top salesperson, instead spending most time with the under-performer in an attempt to raise that person's skill level. The district manager tells the top salesperson, "You don't need my help," knowing that the numbers will come in month after month. At some point, though, even the top salesperson may grow resentful of being ignored so that the boss can spend time with those who contribute less to the market's numbers and company's financial health. Is the distribution of time fair? Whether it is or not, that is usually the way the situation goes. The district manager is responsible for the entire market and must decide where his time is best spent and who needs him most. So goes the daily division for a parent raising multiple children when one has special needs.

In our own family's experience, our younger children were certainly affected by the time I spent focusing on Schuyler. Nearly every weekend for the past six years, I have taken time to visit Schuyler at his residential school. This means a drive as short as 30 miles or as long as 100 miles, one way, which can vary in driving time from half an hour early on a Sunday morning to four hours in a snow storm. And that is just the travel time. While sometimes "we" is just "me" on a day visit, Connor and/or Sloane come along other times. During those visits, we usually get something to eat, take in a movie or an exhibit, check out a bargain shop for some affordable goodies, or look for some other way to seize the day. Depending on the weather or time crunch, we can stretch out the visit and head to the zoo or museum (which made investing in local museum memberships a great deal).

When Schuyler was living in the Hyde Park area of Chicago, we joined just about every museum along the route from our house to the University of Chicago. That meant that at some point during the day visit, we might hit the Adler Planetarium, Shedd Aquarium, Field Museum, Chicago History Museum, or Lincoln Park Zoo. We also became doctorate members of the Museum of Science and Industry (MSI) in Hyde Park, which included free parking on every visit, to make sure that regardless of weather or time, we always had a great option for spending time together. We were lucky to see the Harry Potter exhibit at MSI, have a sleepover at the Field Museum's "Dozin' with the Dinos," and have yet another sleepover at the Adler's "Astro-vernight."

When Schuyler lived just west of Milwaukee, our family became "Wrecking Crew" members of the Harley-Davidson museum. We saw the motorcycle that survived the Japanese tsunami of 2011 and was found intact in a storage container on a beach in Canada 4,000 miles away a year later. We joined the Milwaukee Brewers Kids' Club so we could take fun excursions to local offerings; Connor was in his glory the day we got to walk on the field at Miller Park before a game. Our route to Wisconsin was filled with cool things to do: touring the Jelly Belly factory in Pleasant Prairie (complete with a free bag at the end), stopping at the A&W drive-in (not drive through) in Racine, running around Apple Holler in Sturtevant feeding goats and chickens, dodging apple trees to complete the "cow maze," and enjoying the occasional Green Bay Packers tie-in at McDonalds.

One of our favorite places to visit was a hotel about a mile from Schuyler's group home in Oconomowoc. Over the course of two years, this hotel became our family's own Ronald McDonald House, where we stayed for a night or two at a time. We even spent Easter, Thanksgiving, and Christmas there. (Santa magically found his way to our room!) The hotel was probably designed by a woman who liked to travel with her family—but just didn't want to stay with them. Suites that offered a common living area, fully stocked kitchen, and separate bedrooms with their own bathrooms were the ideal overnight arrangement. Top that off with a hot breakfast buffet—the kids loved making their own Belgian waffle—indoor pool, putting green, fitness center, movie theater, free laundry room, 24-hour pantry and business center, and a beer and wine reception with appetizers heavy enough to serve as dinner, and really, what more do you need? It became a low-key getaway for each of us as we were away from home, in another state, to spend time with Schuyler.

For me, those trips were a simple and fun way to meet all of our needs by making the best of a situation we didn't see ourselves in back in the 1990s. Rather than seeing it as my leaving Connor and Sloane to be with their brother, I could ask, "Hey, who's up for a Culver's run?" and have them spend the day with me as we drove the four-plus hours to and from Wisconsin, stopping at our favorite burger and shake restaurant. Going to a museum or stopping at Goodwill was one way to be with all of the kids, doing what they wanted to do, meeting their need to be with me, and meeting my need for normalcy.

Those are the fun things. But there is another side to this tricky coin.

Many people who don't know us well think we have only two children because Schuyler has lived at boarding schools for six years. Schuyler's challenges can limit our family's ability to be a typical family of five on the most average of days. The kids can become resentful of Schuyler's behavior and the chaos that ensues. They often don't want to have their brother around so he doesn't "ruin" their birthday party or play date. Connor has long been the target of Schuyler's aggression and has incurred many minor injuries over the years from Schuyler's impulsivity. While the bruises and scrapes heal, the experience of having a sibling whose behavior is unpredictable can take its toll on the psyche.

This love-hate relationship is complicated and goes way beyond normal sibling rivalry. Yes, Connor and Sloane love their brother, but they dislike his choices at times. Sloane gets angry (and rightly so) when Schuyler comes in her room and insists on "helping" build her LEGO blocks or stakes a claim on a craft that I bought for her. Sloane has also been exposed to Schuyler's explosive episodes or the aftermath of one. On more than one occasion, she has retreated to her room, covered her ears, and waited for the storm to calm.

On other occasions, I have had Sloane stay at my mom's house nearby during Schuyler's home visits or arranged for her to stay with a friend for two days while I took the boys for an overnight trip. There are times when everyone seems to be at wit's end, and that's when things start to go downhill at warp speed. The simplest comment or action can ignite a response that sends someone over the edge, and we feel as though we have failed, once again, at being a family of five.

But I have to keep trying. I refuse to have one of the kids ask when they are older, "Mom, why didn't you ever do anything to make it better?" We have committed ourselves to healthy bodies and healthy minds, and we are committed to staying intact as a family. Therapy—individual, couple's, and family—has been a mainstay in our home for the past seven years. We engage the talent of school social workers and private counselors, enjoy the release of therapeutic activities, and invite as many other meaningful encounters as we can into our lives.

We use movies and books to start a conversation about lessons that we can use in daily life. The movie *Temple Grandin* was an incredible teaching tool for everyone in our family, as it depicted the way Grandin's brain worked and how her autism allowed her brilliance to translate into our larger understanding of animals. Grandin's social limitations and sensory challenges hit home for us, and seeing her struggle with peers and co-workers gave both Connor and Sloane a much better sense of what Schuyler goes through every day. Sloane has often said, "Autism stinks!" and has asked God why He gave it to

Schuyler. This kind of questioning has cracked the door open to our family uniting behind the common enemy of autism and not Schuyler. Love the brother, hate the behavior, but let's understand why certain things happen.

We also latch on to media coverage of both joyous and difficult events. When Jason McElwain, the boy with autism known as JMac, shot a half-court basket at the buzzer in his high school basketball game, we watched the video on repeat and in amazement. It got a great conversation going at the dinner table about how an illness is not one's identity.

The evening of the dreadful shootings in Newtown, we went around the dinner table to share how we felt. Could it occur here? My God, those poor parents. How can we prevent that from happening again? Our conversation focused on the importance of early intervention for any health concern and the importance of social and emotional support for everyone affected. I was so proud of Connor and Sloane for being able to participate so empathetically. To this day, we make it a point of having dinner together every night, holding hands during grace, and saying at least one thing that we are grateful for that day. It can be as simple as "I got the front seat on the school bus today" to my own, "I'm so psyched that I graduated from my master's program!" Something. Anything. Feeling and expressing gratitude have been some of the tools we use to better understand the hand our family has been dealt and to appreciate that there are millions of other people around the world with greater challenges and far fewer resources to overcome them.

Creating a safe space for healing, problem solving, and just plain bitching is one of the most important things we can do as a family. Each one of us has emotions, concerns, fears, feelings, ideas, and strengths, all of which deserve to be heard, honored, and, if necessary, overcome. At the core of creating this space is the drive to provide our children with the skills they will need as adults, employees, spouses, neighbors, community leaders, and ultimately, parents themselves. Having built a healthy dose of resilience, combined with solid inter-relational skills, is one hell of a foundation with which to tackle what life throws at you.

The Real Deal Takeaway: If you have other children, don't forget that they have real needs that should not be overlooked. Help your other children understand their sibling's challenge, and help them develop empathy for that child's situation. A one-time explanation of your special needs child's condition is not enough. Like the "sex talk," you'll need to layer more and more information as appropriate. We began with "Schuyler's brain sometimes doesn't work right" initially and now can explain that "Schuyler has a mood disorder." Children may not bring up questions if they don't feel the environment welcomes it—but they'll certainly wonder. They may wonder if somehow a sibling's illness is their fault, or if they can "catch" it. In addition to parental explanations, appropriate books, articles, and movies can help children deepen their understanding.

Remember that keeping your family intact and healthy is the ultimate goal. If it helps maintain the peace to let one child stay with friends occasionally to avoid certain family dynamics, that's okay. You do what you have to do, and sometimes avoiding the creation of negative memories is more important than insisting that everyone be together. At the same time, look for activities that inspire all of the kids to want to be together. Know that even the most well planned events can go awry, but focus on the moments of connection that your kids experience, even amongst the chaos. Don't forget to spend individual time with your "typical" children, too, finding out their needs and interests. This can be simply making dinner together or watching a favorite movie on DVD. It's a dance, spending time with each child, as well as the different combinations, but building those positive relationships is essential. And it helps you continuously discover ways to find joy and understanding together as a complete family, if only for fifteen minutes at a time.

"We all have ability.
The difference is how we use it."
—Stevie Wonder

3: WHY MY M.O.M. TRUMPS YOUR M.D.

There is no college where you can earn a degree in parenting. It's the world's toughest, least paying, longest lasting, most panic inducing, future citizens-of-the-world-raising job, and there are zero prerequisites for it. To catch a fish in most states, you at least need to fill out a form and pay fifteen dollars to get a license. Even when applying for a driver's license, you have to pass a vision, written, and road test to prove you can actually drive. The person who does your hair has to be licensed by the state in order to touch your head. But becoming a mother or father? All you need is a space and a few minutes.

Thankfully, nature has equipped even the least initiated of new parents with the internal radar to protect their precious cargo. Enter maternal instinct. Sorry, fathers. It's not that you can't do the job or that you won't do a good job, but we actually grew these people inside our bodies. Many of us fed them with our bodies. And when these sweet and tiny little guys are fresh out of the oven, we have a super hard time being apart from them. We got this one. Don't worry, though, we'll need you more a bit down the road (or just to run out for diapers at midnight).

From the minute the baby is born, something in the maternal brain shifts (let's skip the chemistry lesson, shall we?) into DEFCON 1 mode. The new mom has suddenly morphed into an explosive-detecting K-9 whose infant you bother at your peril. The worldview narrows to a twenty-inch long, seven-pound planet of worry. And that worry, God willing, doesn't stop until you die. Nature wouldn't have it any other way.

Call it a hunch, instinct, or God-given gut check. Most mothers, even if their children are in their sixties, will tell you that they are constantly thinking or worrying about their children. With few exceptions, no person knows them better or can tune in more quickly and accurately to the slightest nuance in emotion. When it comes time to provide information to a school district, piano teacher, or t-ball coach, Mom is there with all the answers (and probably with a few unsolicited thoughts). Keeping the vaccination records, making the growth charts, and taking the pictures (and making the albums) usually falls to the mom. Our closets are brimming with photos of the first day of school, packets of lost baby teeth, and Thanksgiving turkeys made with painted handprints. We have soothed hurt feelings, cleaned up skinned elbows, and cuddled under blankets to share a favorite DVD (for the eighty-seventh time that day) with a sick child home from school. So when it comes to issues surrounding a child's health, moms are the go-to gals.

Years ago, a colleague on a board of directors on which we both served shared with me a comment he heard on his first day of medical school. He said that as the dean spoke to the incoming class, he stated "Half of everything we will teach you is wrong. We just don't know which half." This was at an Ivy League medical school in the 1970s. At that time, medical students were taught that men don't get breast cancer, that the brain does not recover once it is injured, that mental illness is strictly a domain of adulthood, and that autistic meant a person didn't speak. As of 2013, science has proven each of these statements false.

Brain science is evolving at the fastest pace in history, and clinicians must stay current on the latest breakthroughs in diagnosis and treatment. With the mapping of the human genome, researchers are just scratching the surface of solving the mysteries of biology, neurology, and every other aspect of human anatomy. In addition, practitioners also understand that people are not simply comprised of different isolated systems (respiratory, digestive, circulatory) but that every aspect of the mind/body human experience is integrated. We aren't quite there across the board yet, so as consumers, we cannot expect that we will get the same answers and experience with every professional we see. *Caveat emptor*—let the buyer beware—can easily serve as advice for patients or parents seeking clinical clarity.

We turn to medicine for answers, but there are times when we only get more questions, not to mention conflicting conclusions and opinions. Then there are times when we get answers that we instinctively know are either wrong or incomplete. Talk about frustrating. And then there are times when our information or ideas are dismissed. Talk about infuriating! I don't think these practitioners are bad people; I think they have either had limited exposure to what you are presenting to them, have a set way of approaching their patients, or are simply constrained by time or forces at work outside their span of control. But ultimately, as the patient—or the parent of one—you are the coach, and you call the plays.

When Schuyler was around five years old, his right eye became red, painful, and itchy. We saw the doctor on call (not our regular doctor) on a Friday afternoon, and he told us Schuyler had a bad case of pink eye. I knew the doctor was wrong the second the words passed his lips. My gut told me that Schuyler had something beyond pink eye; I just didn't know what. And after all, wasn't the doctor the one who had gone to medical school? We went home with a prescription for eye drops. By dinner, Schuyler's eye seemed worse, and he grew more uncomfortable. I gave him another dose of eye drops at bedtime and hoped his eye would be better by morning. No such luck. A few hours later, Schuyler woke up screaming, and his eye was nearly swollen shut.

At two in the morning, I hurriedly pulled on a pair of jeans and packed up Schuyler for a trip to the emergency room at Evanston Hospital. Sure enough, Schuyler did not have pink eye; he had orbital cellulitis, an infection surrounding his eye socket caused by the cold he had, which had made its way up his nasal passages. It hurt like hell, and the only thing worse than watching the attending physicians try to pry open Schuyler's swollen eyelid was my feeling of regret at taking the pediatrician's word just hours beforehand. I had let his diploma trump mine. I had allowed a lesser diagnosis to override my instinct that something more serious was at hand.

By the time we were admitted to a room on the pediatric floor at sunrise the next day, Schuyler was already on a morphine drip to manage the pain. No amount of trains or trucks could offer him comfort quite like the meds, and all I could do was wait until the antibiotics took hold and rid the body of the inflicting infection. I climbed into the hospital bed with Schuyler, huddled under the covers with him, and tried to recoup some of the sleep I had lost as he watched a Thomas the Tank engine video. By lunchtime, Schuyler's pain had subsided to almost nothing, and the swelling in his eyelid had gone down to a point where he could see a little bit out of the slit the lid could make. After nearly 24 hours of IV drips and a revolving door of residents, we left for home. Pink eye, my ass! Never again would I ignore nature's internal compass.

This commitment would serve me well in subsequent years of working with countless therapists, clinicians, doctors, graduate students, and researchers; while these people knew (or were learning) their respective fields well, I knew my son better. Their professional expertise was no match for my expertise in Schuyler. And none of them could ever care as much about him as I could or be as dedicated to accurate answers and positive outcomes as I was. Any time I heard skepticism from a clinician during the intake process or heard a statement of mine being dismissed as the worries of an overprotective mom, I pushed back. Remember that scene in *Terms of Endearment* when Shirley MacLaine screams at the nurses in the hospital that it's time to give her daughter her medicine, and she runs around to every nurse until the shot is given? There is a little Shirley MacLaine lurking in all parents, ready to pounce on anything or anyone who tries to get between them and their children.

Over time, I learned that if I didn't insist on being heard, I would not be heard. It wasn't about yelling, but about being firm and insisting that my point be at least considered. If there were some new research findings and I didn't ask if a particular treatment might be a good fit for us to try, it might not be brought up. And if I didn't advocate for Schuyler, no one else would. There were times when I taught "professionals" about conditions and treatments. They were experts because they studied a condition; I was an expert because I lived with the condition. I mean, I adore my OB/GYN, but he's never had a baby! Reading and research can take you only so far. So I suppose my only medical credentials are M.O.M. And you know what? That's all I need.

The Real Deal Takeaway: You have earned a doctoral degree in parenting. You know your children best, so never underestimate your expertise when it comes to them. Don't shy away from challenging others as you advocate for what you (and the rest of the team) ultimately want—success as you have defined it. One thing that helped me establish my credibility in the face of skeptical doctors was a huge file with detailed records. I began keeping this file when Schuyler began that first prescription for Risperdal, and I maintain a similar file to this day. It is very difficult to remember what medicines your child may have taken three prescriptions ago, in what doses, and for how long. But when you can calmly look in your file and tell the attending physician that although he might recommend a particular medicine, your child had it in X dose nine months ago and experienced X side effects, it shows you are in control. Having that information clues the "experts" in that you are indeed an expert and should be considered a team member, not hustled off to the side while the doctors do their work.

> "Of all the forces that make for a better world, none is so powerful as hope. With hope, one can think, one can work, one can dream. If you have hope, you have everything."
> —Anonymous

4: DON'T THROW GOOD MONEY AFTER BAD

Baby magazines rarely mention this, but it is really expensive to raise a child. The United States Department of Agriculture estimated that in 2012, it cost more than $160,000 to take care of a child from birth to age eighteen[1]. That's more than $8,000 per year, with the

---

1   http://www.cnpp.usda.gov/Publications/CRC/crc2012.pdf

amount typically increasing as the child ages. That includes housing, clothing, food, childcare, medical expenses, transportation, and miscellaneous expenses (i.e., personal care items, entertainment, etc.). And those are really just the basics. Extras like camp, private school tuition, tutors, sports leagues, school trips, class pictures, school supplies, Girl Scouts, Boy Scouts, babysitters, and birthday parties are not factored in this average annual per-child cost.

Also not included are the extraordinary medical expenses for specialized services such as speech or occupational therapy, individual and family counseling, adaptive equipment, therapeutic aids (such as weighted blankets or picture board makers), respite care, and diagnostic procedures, as well as complementary and prescription medication, especially ones that are too new to come in a generic form. So much of what is required for wellness is not covered by private insurance that parents are left to prioritize what necessities make the cut.

Any family with income limitations must find ways to compromise. But families raising typical children don't have to make these kinds of weekly medical decisions or find creative ways to obtain the services and tangible items they need. I have known of families who contacted a pharmaceutical manufacturer's Patient Assistance Program in order to receive free or discounted prescription medication. Other parents barter with professional providers by doing some bookkeeping or graphic design work for the practice in exchange for treatment sessions. Still other families pool resources to provide respite care in shifts over a three-day weekend or school break. When these types of needs bump up against a family's financial reality, some tough calls have to be made. Competing interests and opposing forces can hurl the most even-keeled parent into a frenzy of choosing what a family goes without in order to make ends meet.

When my kids were younger, a case of Pampers cost $30—almost the same as half an hour of speech therapy. Which one to choose? When the kids got older, should I deny Connor his chance to play t-ball or Sloane a chance to go to summer camp because we'd be spending so much money on Schuyler's treatments? Should Dave and I give up the idea of going out on an occasional date or taking the family on a much-needed vacation because Schuyler's monthly clinical bill needs to be paid? Do we take the younger kids for a quick overnight trip, or do we pay Schuyler's pharmacy bill? Should we take the money for Schuyler's therapeutic residential school and instead offer Connor the opportunity to attend a boarding school to give him a chaos-free environment? How do we make sure everyone's needs are met yet still find balance?

It's natural to go to the ends of the earth trying to find a cure or treatment for a sick child. In the pursuit of relief and normalcy, families understandably leave no stone unturned. Reaching out to physicians around the world, Googling websites at all hours of the day and night, and following every remote lead that might result in "the answer" is more common than not. That quest for wellness, however, opens a desperate family to an unsavory element that preys upon the hope for a cure.

A few years ago, a local hospital began touting a new treatment for kids with autism using a hyperbaric chamber. For a hefty fee, a child could enter the chamber, and the heavier air pressure was supposed to make it easier for that child to breathe in more oxygen, promoting healing. At that time, some professionals in the field viewed this offering with great skepticism, believing that those chambers were simply repurposed equipment that had shown no proof of helping anyone with autism. But families tried it anyway. Parents are desperate for help, and it's hard to say no to what may be "the answer." Most likely, something like this is not the answer, and in order to keep from going bankrupt, we have to set some parameters on what we will and will not do. (For some families, the only result from the hyperbaric chamber was an emptying of their wallets.)

I'm certainly not suggesting that you withhold any treatment for your child, ever. I am saying that we parents need to make smart decisions, even when our emotions are clawing at us. Decide and prioritize what action you will take based on more than just a sense of desperation. Remember when your child was just an infant who couldn't even roll over in the crib, yet you insisted on putting in all the childproof plugs in the outlets, just in case? We want to make sure we've taken care of everything when it comes to the wellbeing of our children, but some things, as in the case of childproofing an infant's room, can wait, at least for a while.

The same can be said for various treatment options; some have a greater sense of urgency than others. Try not to spin yourself into a frenzied ball driving from appointment to appointment, day after day, focused on immediate results. Most therapies take time and are rarely "one and done" kind of deals. And it's not just a matter of money. Even if you have unlimited funds, outcomes are never guaranteed, and some treatments carry with them risk of harm or discomfort during a procedure, or they yield little to no results at all.

Early in my new normal, after we were asked to leave the second preschool program, I was overwhelmed by the long list of treatments I was supposed to pursue and doctors we were supposed to see. Every professional I spoke with directed me to another referral or consultation, much of it not covered by insurance. I was out of answers, out of patience, and soon to be out of money, and I needed to make some serious decisions about our next steps.

Fellow parents are great resources for helping figure out what steps to take first. Be sure to ask what all of your treatment options are; don't assume there is only one. Dig into why families made the decision they did regarding a certain therapy, doctor, or supportive service. In some cases, and parts of the country, there are simply so few places that provide what is needed, you have to take what you can get. Before booking an appointment with any practitioner, check your health insurance plan to see what treatments and conditions are covered by your plan and what professionals are in-network. You don't want to get stuck with an unexpected bill that may take years to pay. For providers that don't take insurance and are only fee-for-service, check to see if you can apply for reimbursement from your Health Savings Account for your out-of-pocket expenses. Something else to consider is the urgency of the treatments being considered. Is there a window of time during which action must be taken or the opportunity is lost permanently? Are there costs beyond treatment, such as airfare, hotel, absence from work, time away from the rest of the family, or missing a special event?

Another thing to consider in beginning or continuing treatment is whether it is effective. Be sure to understand WHY something is being suggested, what behaviors a therapy or medication is designed to target, what potential side effects might arise, and how long until improvement is seen. If—at any point after beginning any treatment—your gut tells you it is not effective or may even be harmful, speak up. Think about how you'll determine whether the treatment is working. What types of changes should you expect to see within what time frame? Not seeing improvement within a realistic time frame may be your cue to stop and reassess.

The Real Deal Takeaway: Instead of spinning the treatment roulette wheel in constant hope that the next spin will land on the magic bullet, carefully consider all of your options. If a suggestion doesn't feel right, you don't have to pursue it. Ask for guidance from other professionals and families, and begin with the possibilities that make the most sense to you. Your child's doctors can be a good resource for helping figure out what steps to take first. Ask them to help you prioritize—which concern is most critical or most time sensitive? Which treatments are covered by insurance? Can you start with those? What is the risk versus the reward of one particular step or treatment? What is the cost of waiting versus doing it now? What is the cost, including travel, and effect on the rest of the family? You're in this for the long haul, so maintaining a sense of personal balance and modest expectations is crucial.

"Where there is no vision, there is no hope."
—George Washington Carver

5: THE ONLY THING CONSTANT IS CHANGE

You've finally established a system. You know how to help your child wake up in the morning and get to school with minimum meltdowns. You have the breakfast she likes ready and her favorite tagless clothes laid out on her bed in the morning. You've become a master at anticipating challenges and avoiding triggers, and you can enjoy a relatively smooth before-school process.

That is, until it all changes. Maybe your child decides she now hates eggs, or maybe her favorite pants are too short after her latest growth spurt. Perhaps the bus driver has been assigned a new route, picking up your child in a different order. Maybe the medicine that worked so well in the past is no longer as effective. Maybe a teacher, doctor, or social worker has quit, left to have a baby, been reassigned, or gotten sick. Regardless of the reason for the change, it can plunge your child into chaos. And your child isn't the only one who is upset. You've spent so much time getting things right, and now you have to start all over again.

As frustrating as it is, that's the reality. We need to remember that things will change. And when that happens, we may need to go back to square one and rebuild. That can be particularly trying in relationships.

Say your son's teacher, the one who really "gets" your son, leaves because his wife just got a job offer on the other side of the country. Now you have to deal with a new teacher who doesn't know your son's background, doesn't understand his tendencies, and doesn't share the same rapport that your son had with the original teacher. The months you've invested educating the original teacher on what works best for your child are lost. Now, you must start all over again with the new instructor, educating her on your child. The nature of the professional fields we encounter is one of frequent change. UGH!

In 2013, Schuyler was assigned a new caseworker for the agency that helps us with the state grant, which pays for a portion of the boarding school tuition. When Jack first contacted me, he began with, "So, tell me about Schuyler."

Really? Did he not have the three-inch thick file on Schuyler's background? All those forms I had spent hours completing for the benefit of those who have permission to view them, and he hadn't taken time to crack it open? Couldn't he at least look through it before calling me? And if he had looked through it, knowing what I was dealing with, could he spare me the effort of updating him on the information he was holding in his hand? To me, Jack was like the doctor who doesn't bother to read your file before walking into your hospital room. It wasn't just the irritation of having to repeat this story; it was reliving all of the pain. The best way I can think to explain it to an outsider is this: Remember the worst day of your life? Maybe it was when you had to put your dog down, or your parent died, or you failed an exam, or someone broke up with you. Okay, are you recalling that? Now, could you tell me everything about that in great detail right now? Would you be up for that, multiple times a month? Probably not, but that is what he was asking me to do in his opening sentence.

My response, I have to admit, was not kind. Maybe he called me on a demanding day. Or maybe it was me pushing back after years of the tribunals of Q&A, interns eager to make mistakes, or giving more of my effort for someone else's benefit. Whatever the reason, I let Jack have it. I told him that in addition to familiarizing himself with clients before introducing himself, it would be helpful for him to lace his conversation with an acknowledgement of the pain the family has experienced. Show some empathy for the situation the family is in, and let them know you get it. The very reason a family is a client is because they have had some kind of unfortunate event befall them or a different kind of trauma. For God's sake, don't be so impersonal and removed! Jack and I actually laugh about it now because, as time passed, we built our own relationship and rapport. He also eventually understood that he should come to me, or any other family, better prepared before the initial contact. Jack now understands why it is important to take the time to read a new client's file or maybe even talk with his predecessor or research a child's illness—anything that might help him become more knowledgeable on the issues a family faces.

The point of this is to accept what we cannot control. Change can happen with little or no warning—school staff get transferred, medications stop working, insurance policies change. Just when we feel as though we have this great routine, with a regimen that is running on all cylinders and a back-up team in place, out comes the rug.

The Real Deal Takeaway: Change is a huge part of our new normal. Sometimes it stinks, like needing to relocate across the country or having your favorite shade of lipstick discontinued, but it can't always be helped. Sometimes we'll handle it gracefully, and sometimes we'll want to pout and wallow in the unfairness of it. And that's okay, for a while. What we *can* do is stop and be grateful for the time we had with a specific person, practice, or event. We can take that experience and use it to build upon our next approach. As we say in our family, don't cry that it's over. Smile that it happened.

"Hope"
—Obama for President campaign slogan, 2008

6: WITH EVERY BREAKDOWN COMES A BREAKTHROUGH

Elizabeth Edwards, the late wife of former North Carolina Senator John Edwards, shared a number of private moments in her book, *Saving Graces*. In addition to letting readers experience the quirky and grueling daily life of a vice-presidential candidate, as well as revealing her intimate struggle to survive breast cancer, Edwards writes most poignantly about losing her son, Wade, in a car accident at the age of sixteen.

Like most (if not all) mothers, Edwards enjoyed a rich and rewarding relationship with her son and was involved in many aspects of his academic and social life. From reading the books in Wade's high school book club with him to hosting his friends at their home for conversation and meals several times a week, Edwards felt a special connection with Wade that many mothers (and fathers) echo.

After Wade died, Edwards writes that for nearly six months, she only watched the Weather Channel. Daughter Cate slept on a chair in the Edwards' bedroom for over a year, and Edwards frequently read to Wade at his gravesite.

During one particular trip to the grocery store, she describes her "Cherry Coke moment." A grocery store is a virtual minefield of emotion for any parent who has lost a child. Every aisle, every display, carries a reminder of the son or daughter or evokes a memory of a time when a certain food was enjoyed. Wade's favorite drink was Cherry Coke. While walking down the soda aisle, Edwards shares in her book, she spots the row of cans, two-liter bottles, and twelve-packs of Cherry Coke, and she loses it. Completely. She is sobbing uncontrollably on the floor of the grocery store in front of the soda display because she came across the Cherry Coke. Edwards wrote that she was so taken with the kindness of those passing by, who offered a word of comfort or just sat with her for a while, and even those who were gracious enough not to stand and stare. Eventually, Edwards was able to stand up and get to her car, still stunned at what had just happened. But she realized she survived a moment she thought she could not.

When *Saving Graces* first came out, Edwards came to suburban Chicago as part of her book tour. On the second floor of the Borders in Deerfield, Illinois, I waited in a very long line to have her sign my copy of her book. As I was nearly last in line, I had the gift of talking with Elizabeth Edwards for a few moments. (Before I could say anything to her, she said "cute shoes," pointing to my black and white floral sandals.) The first thing I said was, "Thank you." But I meant more than an appreciation for the compliment on my shoes.

"Thank you for sharing your Cherry Coke story," I continued. "Knowing of your moment in the soda aisle makes it okay for me to fall apart when my Cherry Coke moment happens."

I told her that because she was so open with her difficulty, grief, and bliss interrupted, she gave me permission to do the same. Edwards listened intently to my sharing a brief version of our family's story, leaning in and asking questions about how we were managing. After the woman behind me in line snapped a photo of the two of us, Edwards offered a hug and words of comfort and inspiration, which were remarkably candid and authentic.

Her vulnerability touched me. I admired her ownership of her experience, the strength to honor her feelings, as overwhelming as they might be, and her decision not to hide from the agony of losing a child. Rather than retreating, Edwards ran into the fire and let those around her express their love and support to guide her through the torment. Her example of grace and courage should be seen as a model for other parents who experience a loss, including those who must mourn the loss of a dream. Raising a child with needs outside the norm—especially when volatile behavior, social stigma, or other uncomfortable facts of life are involved—is, for many, the death of a dream of having the picture perfect family featured on the annual holiday card. Elizabeth Edwards talking about her challenges continues to make the world a better place, allowing parents to share their struggles without fear of being seen as weak-willed or unstable.

As parents, we can look to her example as we tackle the unpredictable nature of our daily lives.

The simple fact remains that our lives do look different from the lives of our friends and neighbors; the sooner we own that, the better. Having awful moments and dreadful days is part of our life for the long haul. On better days, we can see the hand we were dealt with clarity and remind ourselves that everything happens for a reason. We can repeat that God doesn't give us anything we can't handle and thus must think we are strong and great in order to have gifted us with this child. We can believe it when people say, "You guys are the best parents I know" and "I don't know how you do it" and other stuff that sounds great on a Hallmark card. But on other days, I wish someone had told me that it was okay to fall apart, to question God's assessment of my inner strength. On days when the well feels too deep and too dark to climb out, I wish someone would encourage me to become a pile of myself. Some days are just one *diem* I'd rather not *carpe*, thank you.

My own Cherry Coke moments can come in waves and from out of nowhere. If a store clerk gives me a hard time about Schuyler's behavior, my inner bitch can become my outer bitch in a New York minute. When I read about a disabled child who died in the nursing facility that child called home since birth, I grab for my phone to call Schuyler just to hear his voice and tell him how much he is loved. Those Christmas mornings I come down the stairs to see the once-wrapped and tagged presents under the tree unwrapped and all our stockings now unstuffed with goodies spread out across the furniture, I throw up my hands in frustration. No matter what

I do, Schuyler often is simply unable to keep himself from starting his own personal holiday celebration, regardless of how much his actions disappoint his siblings, who anticipate opening their presents on their own. The weeks of planning, shopping, decorating, wrapping, writing, hiding, and staying up past midnight to set the stage for the crack-of-dawn wake-up are gone . . . GONE, in a matter of seconds. On those days, as if I don't already need a nap anyway, it's all I can do to regroup and have Dave keep the younger kids upstairs as I try to re-create Santa 2.0. Rewrapping gifts, restuffing stockings, and disposing of the evidence of the earlier party-for-one leaves me drained, despondent, discouraged, and hardly in a festive frame of mind. This past Christmas, I spent most of the rest of the day in bed, still in my flannel PJs, unable to muster up the energy or interest to do much else. As I channel surfed through the *Christmas Story* marathon, cooking segments with the top five ways to use those leftover cranberries, and ads for after-Christmas clearance sales, I just kept telling myself that we could try again next year.

Too often, I have seen parents put on a brave face and pretend (or deny) that anything is amiss. But you do yourself a disservice when you pass up an opportunity to let the people in your life love you through these character-building moments. (Not that you have to tell every single contact in your address book or post to your Facebook page that you are having "one of those days.") Living in denial is no way to live.

The Real Deal Takeaway: Accept your Cherry Coke moments—and there will be plenty. Turning to your inner circle can mean the difference between getting through a day and giving up. Honor your feelings, own the pain, melt down, and take a nap, in that order. Tomorrow is another day. And remember: that which does not kill us makes us funnier.

"Only in the darkness can you see the stars."
—Dr. Martin Luther King, Jr.

7: IT'S ONLY WEIRD IF IT DOESN'T WORK

Parents, especially mothers, are gifted at thinking through solutions in sticky situations. We must create a Halloween costume out of toilet paper rolls and duct tape, pack up a hotel room in under ten minutes, and save the postgame celebration by snagging cupcakes from the grocery store down the street. We have to create what we need but don't have. Relying on our wit, innovation, and sometimes a shoestring budget, we meet the needs of our family in ways that the marketplace might not have yet conceived. Rather than following the herd during times of high expectations (like holidays), I have found that thinking outside the box works for us, even if it sounds odd to the outside world.

When Schuyler was young, he absolutely loved buttons and knobs. He could spend hours turning anything that had a knob or pressing any button he could find. His favorite place to go was a hardware store to play with locks and touch every single tool kit in the aisles. In my dreams, I would get Schuyler a piece of wood the size of half a door and add to it all the buttons, bolts, locks, hooks, and other hardware available. Playing with small pieces of metal, connecting parts, and placing things in and then out of the same hole for hours was Schuyler's idea of bliss. I can't tell you how many things I've jerry-rigged or created out of desperation. Boxes of packing peanuts, rolls of bubble wrap, and mounds of shredded paper thrilled him. Me, not so much—the cleanup was a bear. But it was worth his entertainment and my sanity, even if it wasn't Toys "R" Us.

Schuyler, like many kids with autism, is sensitive to textures, especially in foods. I wanted him to have solid nutrition, but he refused to eat foods like broccoli, tomatoes, or peaches. Instead of fighting the good fight, I mixed certain pureed fruits (typically baby food) in his favorite foods so he could get the vitamins he needed in a way he would tolerate, as well as not being any the wiser. To this day, I pour a jar of baby winter squash into the sauce when making boxed mac and cheese, add pureed prunes or beets into brownie batter, and sneak a jar of sweet potatoes into the egg wash for chicken strips. Rather than insisting that Schuyler swallow chunks of zucchini, carrots, or bananas, I make a batch of muffins or bread with it instead. If he prefers an applesauce fruit squeezie instead of eating a whole or sliced apple, so what? My goal is to make sure his needs are met, and it doesn't matter if people wonder about my feeding baby food to a teenager.

We generally define successful family time as a block of time when no one is crying or nothing gets broken. We usually have to work at it and plan for it, so I can be assured we will have some time when all five of us are together. When we are at home, the one show we can all agree on is *The Simpsons*, which is guaranteed to calm everyone down and generate laughter. (While I don't love all of the language and innuendos, it's a small price to pay for peaceful and fun family time). We have multiple episodes on the DVR, seasons of DVDs in the car for long trips, and Sloane is fond of her Homer slippers. When we can, we will pile on the couch or bed under a Simpsons blanket with our dog, Scout, and watch enough episodes to bring everyone to a good enough place where we can sit down for a meal—usually pancakes, another unanimous favorite.

One year for Thanksgiving dinner, we stopped in for take-out at Boston Market and brought it to the O School. Another year, we spent Christmas Eve at a hotel in Wisconsin near Schuyler's group home. We sat around in our pajamas and enjoyed frozen pizza and brownies we made in the hotel's convection oven. Thankfully, Santa found us there, leaving our presents and stuffed stockings in the first floor boardroom the next morning! It wasn't a conventional arrangement, but I'm okay with that.

Parents in similar situations typically understand. They've figured out where to buy tagless shirts and seamless socks and how to sew warm lining into coat pockets for kids who refuse to wear gloves during Chicago winters. Moms and dads have figured out the best routes to avoid the Dunkin Donuts drive-through (where not stopping would surely trigger a meltdown), what movie theaters have sensory-friendly show times, and identified which staff in retail stores are most accommodating of requests for assistance. These parents, who ride the challenge wave on a daily basis, often have better solutions than practitioners, who may have the theory but not the practical experience.

We have all learned through trial and error what works for our kids and what doesn't, how to reduce stress and remove triggers we know can bring down the room. A former colleague of mine brought his autistic daughter with him to one of our evening meetings. The wonderful girl was able to wait patiently for about an hour for her dad to finish the meeting by pressing the elevator call button repeatedly. When the elevator doors opened, the girl would walk in and wait for the doors to close, at which point she would press the "door open" button and walk out. She did this for the entire time our meeting was going on. Magic! No one else had to understand why this worked.

The Real Deal Takeaway: Like one ad campaign for a well-known beer states, it's only weird if it doesn't work. You have to find out what works for your family. Don't be constrained by what you think is a "normal" solution to a problem or what a typical holiday should look like. Once you define success on your terms, you will feel more comfortable doing what works, regardless of what friends and neighbors might think. Boston cream donuts are a small price to pay to bring peace and calm to a family, even if it is only for five minutes.

> *"Hope is a good thing. Maybe the best of things.*
> *And no good thing ever dies."*
> —Actor Tim Robbins' character, Andy Dufresne,
> in *The Shawshank Redemption*

8: BEWARE THE MAMA GRIZZLY

Every mother has an inner Leigh Anne Tuohy, or at least they should. The gumption, grit, and outright refusal to accept any nonsense regarding her son, Michael Oher, serves as inspiration for parents around the world. The movie *The Blind Side* famously depicts Tuohy's doggedness in creating a life filled with support, encouragement, and love for another woman's child. What is so fascinating is that Tuohy believes that her life, and that of her entire family, was enhanced in far greater ways by having Oher become part of their family than Oher's life was affected by joining theirs. Tuohy expresses how grateful she is for having met Oher and for having her perspective changed and worldview expanded, adding that her family grew stronger because of the experience. The common bond of having "gone through the trenches with each other" and experiencing things that other families don't go through brought a deeper level of closeness among Tuohy's family of five. A self-proclaimed "strong-willed Southern woman," Tuohy represents what almost every parent is capable of doing on behalf of his or her child, regardless of resources, geography, or challenge.

As I have gotten older, I have come to believe that maternal instinct (or parental instinct) is one of the strongest powers on the planet. The need to protect and provide for people who are utterly dependent on you on a daily basis eclipses even the most urgent external demands. Humans have it, and we see it all across the animal kingdom. Leigh Anne Tuohy is not the exception; she's the rule.

While the Tuohys have financial wealth that may elude the average family, Leigh Anne's mentality of making things happen and shaking complacency lies within the heart of every parent. The day that little soul enters your life, the switch is forever flipped. Ask anyone about his or her lowest moment as a parent, and you will get some revealing answers, including "Which one?" All parents can pull from their memory some occasion during which they believe they failed, they were overcome by enormity of the challenge, or they did not know what to do.

When Schuyler was about two and a half, he hit his head on the bathroom counter. It was during the bedtime routine of brushing teeth, and he was standing on the toilet seat lid when he slipped, smacking his head on the sink and opening the skin above his right eye. After calling a neighbor a few floors below to stay with a sleeping infant Connor, Dave and I took off for our first ER run. As Dave drove, I held Schuyler in my lap with his blanket and stuffed dog—between his bleeding and crying, there was no way I could strap him into his car seat, even for a few minutes. The attending physician examined Schuyler and determined he would need about ten stitches to close the gash. In order for the nurse to sew the stitches, Schuyler was placed on the papoose board, snuggly tucked in as the stitching got underway. I'm pretty sure that I was more of a mess than he was.

Throughout this ordeal, Dave and I tried to keep as calm as possible as we held Schuyler's hand constantly, trying to soothe him and lessen any discomfort. Schuyler was such a champ, but he was clearly distressed, which affected us. At one point in during the stitching, one of doctors said, "You are officially parents!" The confused look on my face, in addition to the exhaustion and exasperation, I'm sure, prompted the doctor to elaborate on what he had just said. "You're not truly a parent until you bring your child into the emergency room," he stated with a confidence that could only have been developed after decades of emergency medicine. The doctor added that having your child hurt, sick, or in pain so severe that you carry them in the middle of the night seeking relief brings out the rawest of human emotions: that of the mama (or papa) grizzly fighting predators that might harm its young. That fierce gut reaction to your child's needs is exactly what nature gave us to make sure the next generation survives; choosing to ignore that instinct comes at our peril.

One thing families like ours have in common is that we are raising children with challenges that cannot be diagnosed by a visual evaluation or any formal DNA testing. We probably have been through at least seven different physicians' offices in hopes of finding the answer that no one seems to want to tell us. For school-aged children, the work ramps up four-fold, as do the demands on kids' time, both in and out of the classroom. Where your son or daughter spends this crucial time can often make or break opportunities for academic, social, or vocational success. Listening to your gut will serve you and your child well as you work to figure out what schools offer the best fit, which professionals offer the most effective treatment, and how to achieve success as you and your child have defined it.

The Real Deal Takeaway: I said before that your M.O.M. (and, yes, D.A.D.) degree is as valuable, if not more, as any other letters before or after your name. But this goes beyond that. No one can fight for your child like you can. No one knows your child better than you do. And no one will ever be as committed to your child's success as you are. Be proud of your inner grizzly.

> "It is virtually impossible to live any kind of
> productive life on this planet without hope."
> —Congressman Emanuel Cleaver II (D-Missouri)

9: ANNE SULLIVAN WAS A SAINT

One of the only bright spots in having a child in special education is having special education teachers and staff in your life. Truly. This amazing group of people woke up one day and decided they would spend their careers with children whose primary needs are not academic and who require intensive, unique, and customized techniques that will demand the best of them every day for decades. There is no phoning it in, no faking it. Special education teachers and staff, in my opinion, do God's work.

Anne Sullivan was Helen Keller's teacher. Keller, who lost her hearing and sight due to an early childhood illness, presented inconceivable challenges to Sullivan. Not only could Sullivan not use textbooks or the spoken word to teach Keller, she had to create a means of reaching her to a point where learning could take place. *The Miracle Worker*, the movie based on Sullivan and Keller's journey, depicts the painstaking attempts by Sullivan to connect with Keller's world of darkness and silence. Using American Sign Language in Keller's hands,

Sullivan broke through countless obstacles that had kept Keller isolated. Through immeasurable frustration and exasperating failures, Sullivan's patience, innovation, and dedication to reaching Keller proved to be the key reason that Keller was able to complete college, travel the world, and ultimately cofound the American Civil Liberties Union. Keller was also awarded the Presidential Medal of Freedom.

Sullivan saw her efforts to reach and teach Keller (which included sitting with her in college classes and signing the lectures to her) as a calling. Despite her own vision loss, Sullivan was able to help Keller see what she could not, hear what she did not, and be part of a world that was entirely separate from her internal one.

Speaking of teaching Keller, Sullivan said, "Every obstacle we overcome, every success we achieve, tends to bring us closer to God." Upon Sullivan's death, the Bishop of National Cathedral (where Sullivan's ashes are interred) stated that the touch of her hand did more than illuminate the pathway of a clouded mind; it emancipated a soul.

My first exposure to special education teachers and staff came when Schuyler started the preschool program through our special ed district. Having been kicked out of two schools before this, I entered the classroom wary but hopeful that this arrangement would work out. I need not have worried. One of the first people I met was Kendra, the speech and language pathologist. A ball of fire, that gal, with such conviction that she was in the exact job she was born to be in! Again, this was a first for me. Kendra introduced herself and immediately told me how psyched she was that Schuyler had joined the class and that she couldn't wait to start working with him. Her enthusiasm was admittedly refreshing, yet it confused the hell out of me. What did she mean when she said she was glad Schuyler was there? Was she really looking forward to spending time with him? What was I missing?

Kendra proved to be the norm within the world of special education. My interaction with her set the stage for working with her counterparts and colleagues throughout the district and state, and it helped me understand what motivates these angels on earth.

One day, Schuyler and I finished a visit at his first therapeutic boarding school, and things hadn't gone well. I was discouraged and disappointed. As I turned the handle on the door to leave, I paused, still reeling from the visit. Then I turned around and asked Ken, one of Schuyler's staff, why he worked there; his response stunned me.

"I feel called to people in pain," he said simply.

"You mean to tell me that you *want* to be here?" I asked incredulously. "Ken, I'm here by chance, but you're here by choice. Why?"

Ken, who holds a master of divinity and looks like he can take down any Navy SEAL, told me how he believes that people in pain, especially children, need and deserve the care, support, and encouragement that will allow them to become who they are meant to be.

Kendra, Ken, and countless others like them amaze me with their career choice. When the rest of the world stares at Schuyler or makes judgments about his behavior, special ed teachers and staff tell me how great he is. These angels on earth want to work with our kids, as unbelievable as that might sound. I have met special ed teachers who tell me that they want the kids who will spit, lick, kick, and bite them. They want the kids who scream, run away, hurl chairs, and throw tantrums on floors. At the risk of sounding like a complete noodge, WHY? There are countless other ways to earn a living or make a difference. Simply put, teaching special education is a calling, a calling for which I'm humbled and profoundly grateful.

The Real Deal Takeaway: As parents of children with special needs, we are so lucky for the Anne Sullivans in our lives. In those moments when I feel I will never reach Schuyler in the way that he needs and that I want, I think of these angels, and I am inspired. The support that special education professionals can provide is truly invaluable. Some parents are initially hesitant to accept help from special ed or dread having their child labeled as special ed. But these folks, by far, are the ones who can provide the community, nurturing, enthusiasm, and support that you and your family need. Seek them out. Thank them. Embrace them. They will embrace you right back.

> *"We make a living by what we get,*
> *but we make a life by what we give."*
> —Winston Churchill

10: HOLLAND ISN'T SUCH A BAD PLACE

Sheila Medow, a beloved former kindergarten teacher of ours, tells her students nearly every day, "You get what you get, and you don't get upset." She may have been referring to getting a red cup instead of a blue one, but the message is the same: you might not like what you got, but you got it. You can get mad and pout, but it won't change the outcome. Instead of getting (or staying) pissed off, tell yourself that while you don't have to like the situation, it's yours. This child has come into your life for a reason, so let's figure out what that reason is.

I didn't have a passport until I was thirty years old. Dave and I met in September of 1997, and our first trip together was a long weekend in London in January 1998. Since I don't subscribe to the thought that getting there is half the fun, I left no detail to chance when planning my first foreign trip. I cashed in airline miles to get two coach tickets to London non-stop from New York's JFK. While I didn't have a clue about what to expect from a pre-9/11 customs checkpoint, I did know that I had to see Buckingham Palace, check out the Food Hall at Harrods, and at least walk by Princess Diana's former home at Kensington Palace. I didn't have to learn any foreign language to get around (although it would have been nice to know that the first floor of a building is not the ground floor), and having English ancestry, I was so psyched about being in the United Kingdom that I could hardly sleep the night before we left.

With all the effort, attention, and excitement I felt about our trip, I would have been horrified to wake up in that final hour of the flight to hear the pilot announce that we were on our final approach to, say, Islamabad. That rude awakening is exactly like the initial stages of learning that your child has autism or a mental illness. All that preparation and anticipation for London, and I'm *where?* I'm sure Islamabad is lovely with a long list of stunning attributes, but I signed up for London. I don't know how to speak Urdu or have any business interests there, and I really, really thought I was on a plane to London. Why am I in Islamabad? How did I get here? Most important, how the hell do I get out?

Emily Perl Kingsley's essay, "Welcome to Holland," so accurately described those emotions. My emotions. Like the woman who found herself diverted to Holland, I found myself in an unexpected life. And it wasn't easy. For years, I was angry, frustrated, and bitter. I was making myself sick. But eventually, I knew I couldn't go on for the next year, five years, twenty years with that attitude, and that I had to change my perspective. While very few of us saw ourselves as parents of children like ours when we were growing up, here we are. And here that child is. Rather than the questions, the what-ifs, and the whys, how about asking "What now?" Choosing to embrace *what is* over *what could have been* is a far healthier way to live in general and especially when it comes to your children. Mrs. Medow would be so proud of you.

The Real Deal Takeaway: Your child's diagnosis is not the end of the world; it's the start of a new one. While you might not like where you are, you're there, and you CAN find beauty in an unexpected place. So, trade in the pasta of Italy for the windmills of Holland, and embrace that where you are is where you are supposed to be. Find a different joy.

"There is always hope when people
are forced to listen to both sides."
—John Stuart Mill

"I sustain myself on the love of friends."
—Maya Angelou

RESOURCES TO MAKE YOUR LIFE A LITTLE EASIER

Special education now encompasses teaching a much broader group of students than in the early days of inclusion. The first wave of legislation, which created the foundation for current law, came in 1974 with the introduction of the Educating All Handicapped Children Act, or EAHCA. The spirit of the bill sought to address some of the gross inequities that some states observed, which prevented some children with handicaps—now referred to as disabilities—from attending public schools. In some instances, parents in certain states could be arrested for attempting to enroll their child in the neighborhood school.

Former Congressman John Brademas (D-Indiana) introduced the EAHCA and oversaw its passage as chairman of the House of Representatives Committee on Education and Labor. Throughout the process, the legislation was intended to ensure that any child, regardless of ability, could receive a formal public education. President Ford signed the EAHCA into law in 1975, which was viewed by advocates (including many parents) as another victory in the battle for civil rights. Coming on the heels of the efforts in the 1960s toward social integration on the basis of race, the EAHCA did for students with challenges what the Civil Rights Act of 1964 did for racial minorities.

In 1990, the EAHCA went through a reauthorization process (which essentially means that Congress agreed to keep funding it), during which the name changed from the EAHCA to the Individuals with Disabilities Education Act, or IDEA as it is commonly known today. One of the central themes of the law was to allow students with challenges to be educated with their non-disabled peers. Advocates and supporters of the law believed it was the right of every child, regardless of ability, to receive a "free and appropriate education" in the "least restrictive environment." Using the Supreme Court decision in *Brown v. Topeka Board of Education* as a template, advocates argued that "separate but equal" education should not be permitted in public schools. The primary reasoning was that having one class for "typical" students and another for "disabled" students was akin to having public schools for white students and other schools for African American students.

With the creation of special education in public schools, districts had to meet the demands of a growing population of students representing many diverse abilities and challenges. The first wave of students to take advantage of the law were students who had previously been excluded from any formal education, due mainly to a mindset of the era which held that those of lesser abilities could best be served in an institutional setting. As such, very little thought had been given to providing a formal education or any kind of vocational training to those living with disabilities.

At that time, one of the biggest challenges was to accommodate the physical needs of students, such as building an entrance ramp and widening doorways for those using wheelchairs. School districts also had to adapt their curriculum to enable students with disabilities to learn while not compromising educational standards.

In addition, schools had to determine the best environment for the student and create an Individualized Education Plan (IEP) that detailed specific strengths and weaknesses of that student. Again, as the definitions of "handicapped" and "disabilities" grew, the number of students who were eligible for support grew with it.

Under current policy, the U.S. Department of Education cites twelve different categories of disability under which a student may receive special education support and services. These categories run the gamut from blindness and speech impediments to autism and emotional disturbance. For each category of eligibility, teachers need a unique skill set to reach and teach these students. Special education teachers and staff are the ones who make public school a reality for over two million students throughout the United States every day.

More specific information, including forms, checklists, etc., is available at the website for the U.S. Department of Education, Office of Special Education and Rehabilitative Services at *http://www2.ed.gov/about/offices/list/osers/reports.html*.

In addition to national resources, each state's education authority has an office that oversees special education on a state level. You can get information about your own state's special education resources by checking out the state board of education. In addition, your local school district has a person or department that is in charge of special education services for any child rightfully living within the district boundaries. Again, look on the district's website for contact information, and make an appointment to discuss concerns, plans, and possibilities for your son or daughter.

REACHING OUT TO RULE MAKERS

One of the most effective ways of changing policy is to contact rule makers directly. At all levels of government, appointed and elected officials have the ability to introduce bills, which can either eliminate negative policy or create positive policy. Since not all lawmakers have your experience, it is important to share your family's story with them.

Depending on the level of government, you will have access to officials within your own town, such as an alderman or member of a city council, or a district office of a member of the state assembly or Congress. Once you know what issue you would like to see addressed, this should tell you what office has authority in that area (for example, the federal government handles Social Security, whereas the state government handles drivers' licenses, and the local government takes care of garbage collection).

Since most governments and officials have dedicated websites, finding who to call for what is pretty simple. A good place to start can be your state board of elections website. By putting in your zip code, you should be able to see what legislative district you are in and access the contact information.

As for what to say, keep it simple and get personal. The key is to let the lawmaker know what is not working in the current law. Ideally, you should also offer a remedy, which doesn't always mean more money. Share how your family has been negatively impacted by a rule on the books or how the lack of a law caused a hardship. Think if it this way: nearly every law in every state and the federal government is a direct result of someone's bad experience.

The Founding Fathers couldn't think of everything! As we grew as a nation, new issues arose, and courts of law and legislatures had to decide how to proceed. With results creating winners and losers, those who had difficult experiences often appealed for amending laws to reflect greater fairness so others would have better outcomes.

Having participated in legislative advocacy efforts for over twenty-five years, I can tell you this: nothing has as great an impact on a lawmaker as hearing from the parent of a child in need. Policy makers must be well versed in a range of issues as diverse as environmental regulation to food safety to banking services. There is no way that every lawmaker can understand every issue, especially when they have not had any personal experience with that issue. Not all lawmakers are parents, so sharing your experiences makes a huge difference.

One of Maria Shriver's brothers, Mark Shriver, served in the Maryland legislature. A while back, I had the privilege of meeting him while he was at The Bookstall in Winnetka to promote the book he had written about their father, Sargent Shriver. After Mark completed his comments, I asked him to sign my copy of his book. I also asked him how a parent could be most effective in talking with legislators. Without missing a beat, Mark said, "Bring twenty other parents with you!" Nothing can take the place of an authentic and passionate conversation about how your daily life is made more difficult by a policy that a government has put in place or a remedy that has not yet been enacted. Mark's comments have been echoed by countless lawmakers, and the collective efforts of parents across the country have resulted in some well-known laws.

The AMBER Alert Program was the direct result of the kidnapping and murder of nine-year-old Amber Hagerman of Arlington, Texas, in 1996. Advocates worked to create AMBER alerts in every state until 2005, by which time all fifty states had formal systems in place. This alert system, which has since expanded to include text messages on personal cell phones, was designed as a rapid response to any report of a missing child, as it is understood that the first three hours of an abduction are the most crucial.

The family of seven-year-old Megan Kanka of New Jersey fought for a law that would let residents know when a convicted sex offender moved into their neighborhood. After their daughter was murdered by a convicted sex offender in 1994 who had moved near their home, the Kankas met with members of the New Jersey state legislature to make sure that any family in the state would have the right to know where anyone with a conviction lives. In 1996, the legislature passed, and the governor signed the bill. Megan's Law has been adopted in every state.

John Walsh might be best known for hosting *America's Most Wanted*, helping catch criminals throughout the country. The reason Walsh became inspired to help put the bad guys behind bars was the 1981 kidnapping and murder of his six-year-old son, Adam, near their Florida home. Following Adam's death, Walsh reached out to lawmakers in the state legislature, as well as to members of Congress, to establish a national database to locate missing children. In 1984, Walsh's efforts resulted in the creation of the Center for Missing and Exploited Children.

While each of these examples might be dramatic, and very tough to read about or remember, it does prove the point that families' voices matter. Each of these laws and organizations are now household names. How did that happen? Someone's horrid experience became the fuel for changing the laws to make sure what happened to them never happens to anyone else. To whom did these families reach out? Lawmakers, as these are the men and women who sponsor, consider, and vote on what laws we live by at all levels of government.

So, when it is your turn to meet with your lawmaker, fear not! It's as easy as 1, 2, 3:

1. Think of three facts to illustrate your point or what obstacle are you encountering.
2. Bring your child with you to help put a face to the issue.
3. Ask for the lawmaker's support by letting him or her know what is in it for them.

So how do you do this in an effective way? Here are some examples.

When calling for an appointment, say that you and your family are constituents and you would like help on a certain issue. Explain briefly what is on your mind, and say that you would appreciate getting some time on the person's calendar to talk through a solution face to face. In my opinion, speaking with local office staff is a bit better than reaching out to the office in the state capitol or in Washington, D.C. Local offices tend to be a bit more focused on serving constituent needs, whereas capitol offices can be more focused on legislation. Again, information on how to contact the local or district offices can be found on the website of your state assembly or state board of elections.

If you prefer to send an email or snail mail letter simply to voice your support or opposition to a bill under consideration, you could write something like:

The Honorable Joanne Smith
Street Address
City, State, and Zip Code

Dear Congresswoman Smith,

Today I write to let you know that I strongly support the bill being considered in the House that would require all public schools to have working sprinkler systems.

My two children attend Mayflower School in Yourtown, and it concerns me that due to its age, the school does not have a sprinkler system. When the time comes to cast a vote on the bill, please vote yes. Our children deserve to be protected during the school day and your support will help ensure that safety.

Thank you for listening and considering my request. Please let me know how I can help in this effort, including joining you at any upcoming committee hearings on this important issue.

Sincerely,

Maggie Cummings
Street Address
City, State, and Zip Code
Area Code and Telephone Number
Email Address

Be sure to call to follow up a few days after sending the letter to confirm with the district office staff that the letter made it. You can also follow up via email to make sure your voice was heard. Since policy makers want to take the pulse of what their constituents—hear what they want or don't want—your input provides great insight.

The easiest way to stay current on any changes to laws that are being considered is to join the email list of an advocacy group's local chapter. This means that you will receive periodic alerts whenever there is a piece of legislation that has been introduced so you can voice your support or opposition to your elected officials.

The best way to find information about your elected officials is to visit these websites:

http://www.house.gov – This is the site for the U.S. House of Representatives. Every family has a representative, or congressperson, in the House of Representatives, who serves a two-year term. Once you are on the site, you can enter your zip code under "Find Your Representative" and viola! There is contact information for the person who is your voice in Washington, D.C. Look for the "district office" information, and you will find that it is probably close to your house. Give a quick call to make an appointment to introduce yourself to the members and their staff. And remember to bring your child!

http://www.senate.gov – This is the website for the U.S. Senate. Every state in the country has two people representing that state, called senators, or members of the Senate, who serve six-year terms. When you are on the site, look for the "Find Your Senators" icon in the upper right corner. Select your state from the drop-down screen, and the names of both of your senators will appear. You can click over to their respective websites.

Again, look for district offices, as there will be many throughout the state. Call the office nearest you and make an appointment to introduce yourself to the senator and his or her staff.

For state government resources, a good place to start is the National Council of State Legislatures at *www.ncsl. org*. Once you are on the site, select your state (in the left column) and select "legislators" (in the right column). Click on "legislative links," and you will find information on your state's house and senate.

You might find that your state senator and representative have district offices very close to your home, which should make it easy to connect with them. Introduce yourself and your child to the legislators and their staffs, offering yourself as a resource to them on issues that concern families in the district.

Also, each state has a state board of elections that can provide contact information for your board of elections director and let you know in what district you reside.

If you live in Nebraska, you have an easier go of it, as you have only the unicameral (lucky!).

Regardless of where you live, every state has elected and appointed officials who make rules that shape how we live our lives on a daily basis. It's important that we let these rule makers understand what obstacles we face and offer potential solutions. Remember—you are the expert, as you live this every day. Share your story with your lawmakers to help them get it right.

FAMILY PRESERVATION

One of the greatest gifts you can give your family is a "rock-star" therapist. Truly. So many issues arise in families like ours that without some solid guidance from professionals who work with families in crisis and know their stuff (and are not afraid to nudge conversations toward resolution), many of us simply break from the strain.

In addition to asking friends for a referral, a good place to start is your insurer's website. If you are insured, check first for family therapists in your network. From there, see which ones are accepting new clients and then call for a brief conversation to discover whether this person might be a good fit for your family. You might consider an initial visit with the therapist prior to bringing in other family members.

In my opinion, the key to finding the right therapist is rapport. You will get into some pretty personal stuff with this person (it's not like changing your oil or doing your taxes), and the only way true emotional intimacy can happen is if you feel a connection with the person shepherding your family through this maze of emotions.

Another good place to find a therapist is *www.good therapy.org*. This international organization offers referrals to a variety of practitioners who adhere to a set of core values in their approach to therapy. Once on their site, you can view their areas of specialty and personal philosophy toward healing.

The American Association of Marriage and Family

Therapy is an additional resource to locate a therapist near you. On the website *www.aamft.org*, members of the association can be found under the "Locate a Therapist" tab. Just type in your zip code and click on a therapist in your area for additional information about credentials, specialties, and licensure.

Keep in mind as you search for the right fit for your family that the person you are entrusting with your family's growth and healing should clearly understand what you experience every day.

Many years ago, we were referred to a therapist to help us work through some of the challenges we faced on a regular basis. During our initial interview, I asked how many children this marriage and family therapist had and how long she had been married. Turns out the therapist did not have children and was single. Now, I'm not saying that this therapist would be unable to help us with our situation or was in any way unqualified. But I was surprised to be referred to someone who had no real-life experience with what we, her clients, needed guidance about. Theory is great, as is research, but at this point in our family's marathon, I knew we needed hardcore answers from someone who was more familiar with our kind of journey.

Developing a positive relationship with a therapist can take time but can be transformational for the entire family. Investing in your family's long-term health and wellness is among the most important decisions you can make. Being able to have clinical guidance and support through both difficult and successful times alike will pay dividends for decades to come. For those family members who might resist, remember that even Olympic athletes have coaches to help them stay at the top of their game.

Asking someone at your house of worship about a support group for families is another route to expanding your circle of support. If no group exists, offer to host a coffee gathering in your home or after services one week for anyone who is interested. Your congregation's leadership should be able to connect you with other families who have expressed an interest in such a group.

Finally, getting a break from the stress of managing daily life is essential for everyone in your family, whether that means having a respite worker take your child on an outing or coming into your home so you can leave. A number of agencies and organizations provide respite care for families, but not all offer the same level of care or work with children.

The best way to find a respite care provider is to start with your own state's respite care coalition or network. Your township or county office should be able to provide you with a referral to a reputable provider located near you. Also, your school district's special education coordinator or park district's ADA liaison should point you in the right direction. Local franchises of national care provider services should also be able to find the right fit for your family.

The most important aspect of finding a good fit is locating someone who has experience with and wants to work with children who have your son or daughter's condition. Many respite workers have experience caring for patients with Alzheimer's disease or age-related conditions, so please keep in mind that one size never fits all, and invest time to find the right person to provide the respite care. Younger caregivers can be a better way to go, both from an energy and physical strength perspective (not that an older person cannot offer the same), since our children are rarely sitting still.

SIBLINGS

To say that the siblings of children with special needs often get the short end of the stick is an understatement. Think about it—if someone in your home gets the flu or breaks an arm, doesn't daily living look different during that time period? Other members of the family must pick up the slack, take on more responsibilities, and put their own plans on the back burner. Extra errands to the pharmacy and home-cooked meals give way to canceled appointments and take-out dinners for weeks on end. As the unaffected family members look on, they keep telling themselves that this is temporary and they are only days away from normal life. But what if that normal life never comes back?

Those families that have both affected and typical children can tell you that out of pure necessity, more time and attention are spent on the sibling with special needs. Regardless of the specific challenge, that child's condition will require additional visits and communication with clinicians, perhaps adaptive equipment (which is not always covered by insurance), and countless hours of a parent's energy. While unaffected siblings might be able to wait patiently until a parent has time for them, the cumulative effect of not being the first to have their needs met can be devastating for the family and for the siblings.

Thankfully, a number of organizations recognize the need for normalcy for children who have siblings with special needs. Among the most recognized is the Sibling Support Project, created by Don Meyer. Over the years, Don has presented workshops internationally and has created Sibshops: workshops for brothers and sisters of children with special needs. More information is available on his website, *www.siblingsupport.org* and at *http://plus.calendars.net/sibshop*. Don has also authored the following books:

- *Uncommon Fathers: Reflections on Raising a Child with Special Needs*
- *Living with a Brother or Sister with Special Needs: a Book for Sibs*
- *Views from our Shoes: Growing Up with a Brother or Sister with Special Needs*
- *The Sibling Slam Book*
- *Thicker than Water: Essays by Adult Siblings of People with Disabilities*

To find a Sibshop near you, here are several ways to connect with Don.

Don Meyer
Director, Sibling Support Project
A Kindering Center program
6512 23rd Ave NW, #213
Seattle, WA 98117
Phone 206-297-6368; fax 509-752-6789
donmeyer@siblingsupport.org

Regardless of how you actively support your typical children, please know that while their needs are not as apparent as your affected child, they need you just as much. Over the years, I have spoken with many adults who grew up with a sibling with special needs, and their experiences usually fall into one of two camps: some saw the challenges their sibling faced every day and eventually pursued a role within special education or some therapeutic environment, while others felt a huge sense of resentment that their parents constantly ignored their needs by focusing only on their affected sibling. While most in the second camp admitted that they understood their sibling's treatment required a greater share of resources, most felt shortchanged. One woman told the story of how her parents were always bailing her affected brother out of a problem of his own creation, which left little to no money for her to enjoy the occasional indulgence.

Also, in both camps, adult siblings expressed a genuine concern that their affected sibling would ultimately become their responsibility once their parents died. Most adult siblings said that they had not had conversations with their parents about such arrangements and were unsure if financial provisions had been made for their affected sibling. Every family should have a substantial conversation about this. A number of outstanding, reputable financial planners specialize in creating special needs trusts and other tools to ensure that every member of the family can participate in future financial protection.

If your typical children are in grades K–12, chances are their school has a social worker they could talk to regularly as part of the support they receive in school. Also, having an activity all their own, like a sport or club, can do wonders for their self-esteem. Keeping a journal handy to jot down feelings (good and bad), draw pictures (good and bad), and record miscellaneous thoughts can be an easy and inexpensive way to equip typical siblings with a simple outlet to vent. It is very helpful when siblings can get together with other kids their age who have similar siblings; they can hang out with each other, share stories, and create a supportive friendship with someone else who really gets what their life is like.

Again, do the best you can with what you have. There is no right or wrong way.

ADDITIONAL RESOURCES

The Complete Guide to Special Education: Expert Advice on Evaluations, IEPs, and Helping Kids Succeed, second edition, by Drs. Linda Wilmshurst and Alan Brue, is a great guide to keep handy throughout the school year, as it provides current information on the various aspects of special education.

As you might have already learned, different organizations offer and specialize in different things. Some organizations focus on research, while others offer support and referrals. Knowing that there are so many resources available can be overwhelming at first, so here are some good places to start:

The Balanced Mind Foundation
http://www.balancedmind.org

Mental Health America
http://www.mentalhealthamerica.net

National Alliance on Mental Illness
http://www.nami.org

Autism Speaks – The 100 Day Kit is specifically designed to support families of the newly diagnosed.
http://www.autismspeaks.org

The Autism Society
http://www.autism-society.org

Each of these organizations has a section on its website that allows you to locate in-person support groups, educational workshops, and even clinician referrals in your area. Also, you can find chat rooms on social media for each of these groups, in addition to peer support for specific areas of interest.

Autism Research Institute
http://www.autism.com

Dr. Temple Grandin – Dr. Grandin has numerous resources on her website, including sensory products.
http://www.templegrandin.com

Dr. Oliver Sacks
http://www.oliversacks.com

Andrew Solomon – Dr. Solomon is the author of *Far From the Tree*, a magnificent book about parents who have children who are vastly different from them (hence, the apple *does* fall far from the tree).
http://www.andrewsolomon.com

My hope in creating this book is that you feel less alone and stronger in spirit after reading it. I hope you have a better sense of what you can expect in the years to come . . . and I hope you are starting to know you will be okay.

Back in 2002, I needed this book, or at the very least another person in my shoes who would go out for coffee with me and tell me what I needed to know and not what I wanted to hear. In the beginning, I was so solitarily desperate for answers and meaning that I exhausted myself. I hope you finish this book with a renewed reason to smile. More acceptance and less anger. Fewer *what ifs* and many more *what nows*.

A compass for your new normal is now in your hands.

If you find anything in these pages that has been particularly valuable to you, please consider reaching out to others in similar circumstances and offering some comfort as they try to push through a tough time. Doesn't it feel great when someone does that for you?

I hope our paths cross soon. Until then, remember: you are stronger than you know.

Cheers!
Christine

*"The one unchangeable certainty is that nothing
is certain or unchangeable."*
—John F. Kennedy

ACKNOWLEDGMENTS

The group of visionaries at Round Table Companies took my story and gave it wings. The authenticity, devotion, commitment, expertise, empathy, direction, patience, love, and joy that every member of the RTC team brought to the process of making this book a reality is humbling. Corey Blake, David Cohen, Erin Cohen, Kristin Westberg, and the writing/editing team of Katie Gutierrez and Pamela DeLoatch are thought and action leaders who serve as role models for other companies championing people's lives. Thank you for gently holding my heart in your hands and not laughing or judging when you heard the good, the bad, and the ugly.

To my family. My husband Dave, my other half for 15 years now: I love you more than I'm able to express. While I had no idea what a wild ride we would be in for when we met back in September of 1997, I couldn't imagine taking the ride with anyone but you. Thanks for asking—and I'm still glad I said yes. Schuyler, Connor, and Sloane, you are the reason I do everything I do every day. I'm so happy to be your mom. You will never know the joy and privilege I feel having you as my children. Thanks for coming! And my amazing mom, Joan. Where would I be without you? You made it possible for me to get here. Period. How does one top that? Your courage, smarts, support, modeling, choices, perseverance, and humor made me what I am today. Love you bestest, mostest!

And to my incredible circle of friends. You know who

you are! Thank you for enduring my unreturned phone calls and emails while I was pushing through my writing deadlines and for still talking to me when I came up for air. Your love and support nudge me through the awful moments, and your cheering helps me go just a little further, just when I think I cannot. You are my GPS.

> *"Those things we regarded as our greatest misfortunes have proved our greatest blessings."*
> —George Mason, 1785

CHRISTINE WALKER, MPPA

BIOGRAPHY

Christine Walker's background is in public policy. Prior to becoming a parent, Christine worked with government leaders in Washington, D.C., Illinois, and Ohio. As such, Christine brings her unique experience with disabilities to the public policy arena.

Following an award-winning career with Tiffany & Co. Business Sales, Christine returned to her policy roots once her family's challenges became apparent. Christine is a dedicated advocate for children's mental health and works tirelessly to educate policymakers to enhance the lives of families raising children with hidden disabilities.

In the past, Christine has attended the invitation-only Rosalynn Carter Mental Health Symposium at the Carter Center in Atlanta with fellow professionals and advocates. Also, Christine has attended the One Mind for Research conference held at UCLA and is involved with the Illinois Mental Health Summit. Christine also serves on the New Trier Township Committee on Disabilities, working toward enhancing the lives of those living with disabilities in her community. Additionally, Christine has served as a teaching assistant for a course on the legislative process at Northwestern University.

In 2004, Christine had her first book published. *The Smart Mom's Guide to Staying Home: 65 Simple Ways to Thrive, not Deprive, on One Income* shows families how to live well for less. Christine and her book were profiled on *Fox and*

Friends, CLTV's "Your Money," WGN, the *New York Times*, *Parade*, *Chicago Tribune*, and other publications.

Christine holds a Masters of Public Policy and Administration from Northwestern University and a BA in Political Science from Lake Forest College. She lives in Winnetka, Illinois.

If you would like to contact Christine, please visit *www.chasinghope.com*. Chasing Hope, LLC is a consulting firm which supports families raising a child with autism and/or mental illness. You can also follow her on Twitter: *@chasinghope2014*.

PAMELA DeLOATCH

BIOGRAPHY

Pamela DeLoatch is a writer, editor, and storyteller. With a journalism degree from American University and an MBA from Duke University's Fuqua School of Business, Pamela crafts writing to educate, entertain, and engage. She is delighted to be part of this special project to help increase education and compassion for children with special needs and their families.

ABOUT ORP

Oconomowoc Residential Programs, Inc. is an employee-owned family of companies whose mission is to make a difference in the lives of people with disabilities. Our dedicated staff of 2,000 employee owners provides quality services and professional care to more than 1,700 children, adolescents, and adults with special needs. ORP provides a continuum of care, including residential therapeutic education, community-based residential services, support services, respite care, treatment programs, and day services. The individuals in our care include people with developmental disabilities, physical disabilities, and intellectual disabilities. **Our guiding principle is passion:** a passion for the people we serve and for the work we do. For a comprehensive look at our programs and people, please visit *www.orp.com*.

ORP offers two residential therapeutic education programs and one alternative day school among its array of services. These programs offer developmentally appropriate education and treatment for children, adolescents and young adults in settings specially attuned to their needs. We provide special programs for students with specific academic and social issues relative to a wide range of disabilities, including autistic disorder, Asperger's disorder, mental retardation, anxiety disorders, depression, bipolar disorder, reactive attachment disorder, attention deficit disorder, Prader-Willi syndrome, and other disabilities.

Genesee Lake School is a nationally recognized provider of comprehensive residential treatment, educational, and vocational services for children, adolescents, and young adults with emotional, mental health, neurological, or developmental disabilities. GLS has specific expertise in Autism Spectrum Disorders, anxiety and mood disorders, and behavioral disorders. We provide an individualized, person-centered, integrated team approach, which emphasizes positive behavioral support, therapeutic relationships, and developmentally appropriate practices. Our goal is to assist each individual to acquire skills to live, learn, and succeed in a community-based, less restrictive environment. GLS is particularly known for its high quality educational services for residential and day school students.

Genesee Lake School / Admissions Director
36100 Genesee Lake Road
Oconomowoc, WI 53066
262-569-5510
http://www.geneseelakeschool.com

T.C. Harris School is located in an attractive setting in Lafayette, Indiana. T.C. Harris teaches skills to last a lifetime, through a full therapeutic program as well as day school and other services.

T.C. Harris School / Admissions Director
3700 Rome Drive
Lafayette, IN 47905
765-448-4220
http://tcharrisschool.com

Transitions Academy provides behavioral health and educational services to adolescents in a 24-hour structured residential setting. Treatment services are offered that are best practice and evidence based, targeting social, emotional, behavioral, and mental health impairments. Transitions Academy serves children from throughout the United States.

Transitions Academy / Admissions Director
11075 North Pennsylvania Street
Indianapolis, IN 46280
Toll Free: 1-844-488-0448
admissions@transitions-academy.com

The Richardson School is a day school in West Allis, Wisconsin that provides an effective, positive alternative education environment serving children from Milwaukee and the surrounding communities.

The Richardson School / Director
6753 West Roger Street
West Allis, WI 53219
414-540-8500
http://www.richardsonschool.com

FAMILY SUPPORT

Schuyler Walker was just four years old when he was diagnosed with autism, bipolar disorder, and ADHD. In 2004, childhood mental illness was rarely talked about or understood. With knowledge and resources scarce, Schuyler's mom, Christine, navigated a lonely maze to determine what treatments, medications, and therapies could benefit her son. In the ten years since his diagnosis, Christine has often wished she had a "how to" guide that would provide the real mom-to-mom information she needed to survive the day and, in the end, help her family navigate the maze with knowledge, humor, grace, and love. Christine may not have had a manual at the beginning of her journey, but she hopes this book will serve as yours.

CHASING HOPE
YOUR COMPASS FOR A NEW NORMAL
NAVIGATING THE WORLD
OF THE SPECIAL NEEDS CHILD

ASPERGER'S DISORDER

Meltdown and its companion comic book, *Melting Down*, are both based on the fictional story of Benjamin, a boy diagnosed with Asperger's disorder and additional challenging behavior. From the time Benjamin is a toddler, he and his parents know he is different: he doesn't play with his sister, refuses to make eye contact, and doesn't communicate well with others. And his tantrums are not like normal tantrums; they're meltdowns that will eventually make regular schooling—and day-to-day life—impossible. Both the prose book, intended for parents, educators, and mental health professionals, and the comic for the kids themselves demonstrate that the journey toward hope isn't simple . . . but with the right tools and teammates, it's possible.

MELTDOWN

ASPERGER'S DISORDER, CHALLENGING BEHAVIOR, AND A FAMILY'S JOURNEY TOWARD HOPE

MELTING DOWN

A COMIC FOR KIDS WITH ASPERGER'S DISORDER AND CHALLENGING BEHAVIOR

AUTISM SPECTRUM DISORDER

Mr. Incredible shares the fictional story of Adam, a boy diagnosed with autistic disorder. On Adam's first birthday, his mother recognizes that something is different about him: he recoils from the touch of his family, preferring to accept physical contact only in the cool water of the family's pool. As Adam grows older, he avoids eye contact, is largely nonverbal, and has very specific ways of getting through the day; when those habits are disrupted, intense meltdowns and self-harmful behavior follow. From seeking a diagnosis to advocating for special education services, from keeping Adam safe to discovering his strengths, his family becomes his biggest champion. The journey to realizing Adam's potential isn't easy, but with hope, love, and the right tools and teammates, they find that Adam truly is *Mr. Incredible*. The companion comic in this series, inspired by social stories, offers an innovative, dynamic way to guide children—and parents, educators, and caregivers—through some of the daily struggles experienced by those with autism.

MR. INCREDIBLE

A STORY ABOUT AUTISM, OVERCOMING CHALLENGING BEHAVIOR, AND A FAMILY'S FIGHT FOR SPECIAL EDUCATION RIGHTS

INCREDIBLE ADAM AND A DAY WITH AUTISM

AN ILLUSTRATED STORY INSPIRED BY SOCIAL NARRATIVES

BULLYING

Nearly one third of all school children face physical, verbal, cyber, and social bullying on a regular basis. For years, educators and parents have searched for ways to end bullying, but as that behavior becomes more sophisticated, it's harder to recognize and to stop. In *Classroom Heroes* and its companion comic book, Jason is a quiet, socially awkward seventh grade boy who has long suffered bullying in silence. While Jason's parents notice him becoming angrier and more withdrawn, they don't realize the scope of the problem until one bully takes it too far—and one teacher acts on her determination to stop it. Both *Classroom Heroes* and its companion comic recognize that in order to stop bullying, we must change our mindset. We must enlist not only parents and educators but the children themselves to create a community that simply does not tolerate bullying. Jason's story demonstrates both the heartbreaking effects of bullying and the simple yet profound strategies to end it, one student at a time.

CLASSROOM HEROES

ONE CHILD'S STRUGGLE WITH BULLYING AND A TEACHER'S MISSION TO CHANGE SCHOOL CULTURE

CLASSROOM HEROES

COMPANION CHILDREN'S BOOK

REACTIVE ATTACHMENT DISORDER

An Unlikely Trust: Alina's Story of Adoption, Complex Trauma, Healing, and Hope, and its companion children's book, *Alina's Story,* share the journey of Alina, a young girl adopted from Russia. After living in an orphanage during her early life, Alina is unequipped to cope with the complexities of the outside world. She has a deep mistrust of others and finds it difficult to talk about her feelings. When she is frightened, overwhelmed, or confused, she lashes out in rages that scare her family. Alina's parents know she needs help and work endlessly to find it for her, eventually discovering a special school that will teach Alina new skills. Slowly, Alina gets better at expressing her feelings and solving problems. For the first time in her life, she realizes she is truly safe and loved . . . and capable of loving in return.

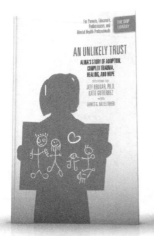

AN UNLIKELY TRUST

ALINA'S STORY OF ADOPTION, COMPLEX TRAUMA, HEALING, AND HOPE

ALINA'S STORY

LEARNING HOW TO TRUST, HEAL, AND HOPE

Also look for books on Prader-Willi Syndrome and children and psychotropic medications coming soon!